Acting Out Your Christianity

An Introduction to the Themes, Theology and Thoughts of Luke-Acts

Every blessing

Chris.

Dr. Chris Palmer

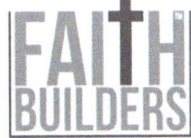

FAITH
BUILDERS

Copyright 2020 Dr Chris Palmer

Faithbuilders Publishing Limited
12 Dukes Court, Bognor Road
Chichester
PO19 8FX
United Kingdom

Tel: 01932 845 296
E-Mail: editor@faithbuilderspublishing.com
www. faithbuilderspublishing.com

First Published in United Kingdom, 2020

British Library Cataloguing-in-Publication Data. A catalogue record for this book is available from the British Library

ISBN: 978-1-913181-52-9

Cover Design by Mathew Bartlett
Cover Image © Alexandr Koltukov | Dreamstime.com
Formatted by Faithbuilders Publishing
Printed in the United Kingdom

Contents

Part 3: Acts Today

Part 1

The Foundation for Our Actions: Luke-Acts

Introduction

The first account I composed Theophilus, about all that Jesus began to do and teach
Acts 1:1

The centrality of the Lord Jesus Christ is the vital element in true Christian Discipleship, and in the effective ministry of the local Christian community. The verse quoted above sets the tone for the whole of Luke's writings, in that it introduces the paradigm of Jesus at the centre of the Christian experience both individually and corporately. As Luke 1:1 sets out the author's intention to record an accurate history of the life, ministry and on-going impact of Jesus, Hans Conzelmann writes:

> The truth is that in the life of Jesus in the centre of the story of salvation a picture is given of the future time of salvation – a picture that is now the ground of our hope.[1]

Conzelmann's sentiments are true as the church looks for salvation to be fulfilled in the person of Jesus Christ; this has been the Christian's hope for 2000 years. Luke is intent on placing the emphasis upon the words and works of Jesus for the reader to discover the principles central to biblical, evangelical, apostolic Christianity. Once these principles have been ascertained it is essential that they are applied to the individual disciple and the corporate body of Christ. Their application is necessary in order to fulfil the on-going purposes of God in the world through the church. A church consisting of individuals who are constantly: 'Acting out your Christianity' the life of discipleship is to be one of action not idleness, engagement not ostracism and proactive not reactive attitudes.

The purpose of this book is to introduce the salient points of Lukan thinking as it relates to the ministry of the local Christian community in the 21st century. Luke's thinking will be examined in a thematic manner and not as a verse by verse analysis of the text. It is presented as a tool for use by local churches in order to gauge their effectiveness after considering the biblical narrative. These

---

[1] Hans Conzelmann, *The Theology of Saint Luke*, (London: Faber and Faber, 1961), 36-37.

themes could further be designated as 'the things that disciples and churches do in their worship and ministry'. It must be highlighted that I consider worship to be a whole of life event and not restricted to twenty-five minutes in a gathering singing. Hence, there is a need for the 21st century disciple to re-evaluate whether they are endeavouring to attract people to a church system or attract people to a life of Christlikeness. The principles in this book, I hope, will be relevant to producing Christ-like disciples fulfilling their calling to go into the world and not sit in their seats and enjoy the entertainment that much Christian worship has degenerated into.

There is a plethora of excellent commentaries available on Luke and Acts that deal with the detail of the text and draw scholarly conclusions.[2] This book stands as a guide to understanding early church practice and interpreting them for 21st century worship. I hope that this book serves as an aid to those involved daily in promoting the gospel and leading the local Christian community. I also offer this book to those everyday disciples who are, along with the many who have trodden this path before, simply endeavouring to know, love and serve God. Each chapter finishes with a 'Think It Over' section which has a few questions to help the reader reflect on the subject discussed.

The foci of this book are the two volumes traditionally held to be of Lukan authorship:

1. The Gospel according to Luke.

2. The Book of the Acts of the Apostles.

It is essential for the modern reader to understand the composition of what the Christian Bible records as two volumes. It is unfortunate that in the biblical canon, or 'rule/authoritative books', the Gospel of John is placed between the two as this disrupts Luke's flow. In dealing with the connection of the two volumes, Richard Pervo writes:

> One thing is certain: the author never intended Luke to be read as one gospel among others, for his aim was to supersede Mark and Q, while Matthew and John were probably unknown to him.[3]

---

[2] See the bibliography for further details.

[3] Richard I. Pervo, *The Gospel of Luke,* (Salem OR: Polebridge Press, 2014), 2.

I concur with the kernel of Pervo's thinking here and submit that when engaging with the gospel of Luke, the reader does not ignore Acts, as they should be read as one continuous document charting the development of the Christian gospel and embryonic church. Further it was Luke's intention that his volumes would present the total picture of the emergence of the Christian religion in the world. As a result, the reader can engage with the mission of God in the world through the church as a fulfilment of the promise to Abraham in Genesis. 12:3 that; *'in you all the families of the earth will be blessed.'* Luke's gospel introduces the reader to the centre of the gospel message and Acts serves as an illustration of the practical application of the theology presented by Jesus and the New Testament Apostles. When read it is possible to construct a clearer picture of the author's intentions, distinctive characteristics and interests. Darrell Bock summaries it thus:

> Our goal in this look at Luke-Acts is to reconnect the volumes to each other and to tell Luke's theological story in which one cannot see Jesus without understanding the story of the community that he was responsible for launching.[4]

I would go one step further than Bock and submit it is also necessary to uncover the principles of the establishment of that embryonic community and apply them to modern church praxis. It is my hypothesis that this understanding will help today in shaping the local church for it to become more effective in its ministry.

There are twelve specific themes that I will highlight in order to trace the theological emphasis of Luke-Acts; these will be discussed in Parts 2, 2A and 2B. Part 1 is the introductory section with Part 3 offering some brief concluding thoughts on the importance of Luke-Acts for today.

Salvation History

By using a series of themes Luke-Acts is providing a summary of 'heilsgeschite' or salvation history. The major theme being the salvation of God offered in Christ to the world through the church. The reader is presented with a continuation of the narrative of the elect people of God now found within the church of the Lord Jesus Christ. Luke develops this central theme by

---

[4] Darrell L. Bock, *A Theology of Luke and Acts,* (Grand Rapids: Zondervan, 2012), 28.

highlighting other subsidiary themes that point to the overarching theme of salvation. Luke's work consists of two main divisions:

1. An outline of the life and ministry of Christ: salvation introduced to the world.
2. An outline of the embryonic Church: salvation presented to the world.

Luke-Acts presents how the whole of salvation history rests in the plans and purposes of God. The scene is set by Luke as he records the announcement of the birth of Jesus in Luke 1:31-33:

> *And behold, you will conceive in your womb and bear a son, and you shall call his name Jesus. He will be great and will be called the Son of the Most High. And the Lord God will give to him the throne of his father David, and he will reign over the house of Jacob forever, and of his kingdom there will be no end.*

The introduction of the gospel calls attention to the 'Most High' God who is the instigator of the salvation plan which has eternal consequences. Therefore, the Christian both individually and in community must depend upon God in order to know salvation and meet the challenges of everyday life. The author presents a very practical document which should help the disciple understand how their forefathers coped in a world which was suspicious of the new sect and at times faced severe persecution. 21st century Christianity is faced with similar issues; scepticism, atheism, post-modern thinking and violence all affect Christian believers today. How the early disciples coped with similar issues should help the modern disciple face the challenges and succeed.

Chapter 1

Why Do I Need Theology?

Now…they received the word with all eagerness, examining the Scriptures daily to see if these things were true. Acts 17:11

'Theology; oh no that's not me!' Most disciples are turned off by the mention of the word 'theology' however, any interaction with the biblical narrative and especially salvation through faith means every believer has engaged with the heart of theology: justification by faith. Therefore, I submit it is essential for all disciples of Jesus to engage with theology to enhance their discipleship and ability to witness to the truth of the gospel. What the church needs is pastors and teachers who are willing to know the truth of theology, live the truth and preach the truth. Therefore, Luke-Acts is pivotal to the 21st century church as there is the presentation of theology and its application. Luke-Acts engages with the main areas of Christian theology and reveals how the local church acted out that theology in the world.

Those mentioned in Acts 17:11 were citizens of the city of Berea in Macedonia; they were Jewish inhabitants who had heard the Christian message through the ministry of Paul. They teach an important lesson to all who are endeavouring to acquire the truth about God, humanity and salvation; search the Bible. This is the divinely preordained method by which the individual can come to a correct knowledge of God. Today we know the study of God as theology which is derived from the Greek word *theologia* which means an account or discourse about gods or God. In Christianity this applies to the investigation into the divine being portrayed or revealed in the Christian Bible; that entity the Christian disciples refers to as God. As the New Testament (NT) writers and disciples were largely of Jewish descent the influence of the Old Testament (OT) view of God is essential in seeking to understand the complete or full revelation of the God in the NT. The serious student of the nature and purpose of God should not neglect the OT as within it are found some of the primary revelations of God to humanity. These revelations coupled to the NT revelation through the person of Jesus and the work of the Holy Spirit bring to view a complete picture of the Christian God. This God is revealed in three persons; Father, Son and Holy Spirit; each of these essential beings has a particular role in the creation and in the revelation of the divine standard to humanity.

Theology can be defined as:

> 'The investigation of the self-revelation of God through the means of biblical study'.

Why Study Theology?

The Bible contains the information that the theologian should collect, authenticate, arrange and present in order to provide a picture of God. This requires a survey of both OT and NT; it is poor methodology for the seeker to ignore the OT revelation of God. The essence of the being and person of God are revealed from the first verses of Genesis and culminate in the visions and intricacies of Revelation. John 5:39 records the words of Jesus to aid one's understanding of the relationship between the OT and NT:

> *You search the scriptures* (our OT) *because you think that in them you have eternal life; it is these that testify about me.* (emphasis added)

In the true pursuit of a knowledge of God it is necessary to unite the OT and NT in order to produce a picture of the Lord the provider of salvation. This includes an understanding of the three persons of the Trinity; Father, Son and Spirit all of whom are essential in one's spiritual quest. Luke-Acts engages with each of the three persons of the Trinity to present enough information to construct a clear picture of God, humanity and salvation.

This revelation of God further highlights the impact made upon the individual and the local Christian community. Luke wants to provide a picture of a God who through the revelation of Jesus Christ by the power of the Spirit can impact both individual and society. Examining Luke-Acts in a thematic manner will bring to light the systematic foundation upon which the Christian Faith is built. It is essential that the facts be shown in their harmony and consistency, from a biblical perspective and that they are applied to the local church community in the 21st century.

It is vital to address theology through the means of the Bible. Many people are put off the study of theology fearing that it is the preserve of stuffy old Bible college professors or pastors and has little relevance to their everyday existence.

However, this is a popular misconception; theology is applicable to all whatever one's level of biblical knowledge[5]. If a person admits to being, a disciple of Jesus they have engaged with theology at its essential point, i.e. knowing Jesus Christ as Lord and saviour. The ultimate purpose of theological discovery is to know God in a personal manner; this is a process that takes many years as there is so much which is vital in one's understanding of God. Hence all Christians are theologians of the word and works of God, learning of God and applying that knowledge to everyday living. It is essential that every student of the Bible applies the knowledge gained within their personal context, otherwise, learning serves simply to fill the head with knowledge and has no helpful consequence. An important principle to remember is 'the goal of Bible study is not simply learning, it's living.'

The individual who desires to discover more of God, to understand the divine plan as set out in the Bible and to know God in a personal manner; should take the study of theology seriously. Conversely the theologian should make theology accessible to all; I have read and re-read some theologies and been left cold or confused. I admit there are some difficult subjects but my plea to theologians is 'make it readable'![6] It can be the case that individuals endeavour to learn about God from different sources especially in our 21st century culture; sadly this can take people away from the revelation of God to the humanistic thinking and produce a distorted picture. It is essential for a true understanding of the God of the Christian Bible to engage with the text that reveals the nature and purposes of God to humanity.

Divisions of Christian Theology

Theology consists of the following major divisions all impacting the true disciple of the Lord Jesus Christ. All are found in Luke-Acts, all are essential in the spiritual development and growth of the disciple of Jesus. Do not be put off by the theological terminology but consider the content of each division and then realise how it impacts your personal experience.

---

[5] Kevin Vanhoozer and Owen Strachan, *The Pastor as Public Theologian,* (Grand Rapids: Baker, 2015), for a challenge for local church pastors to recover their major purpose of bringing theology to the 'everyday Christian'. See also Kevin Vanhoozer, *Hearers and Doers,* (Lexham Press, 2019).

[6] I highly recommend Wayne Grudem, *Systematic Theology,* (Leicester: IVP, 1994), as a very readable book.

1. Theology proper: Godhead, three distinct persons equal in power and glory.
2. Anthropology: origin and nature of humanity, the fall and sin.
3. Soteriology: God's purpose and plan of salvation.
4. Pneumatology: the essential person and work of the Spirit.
5. Ecclesiology: nature, purpose and function of the Church.
6. Eschatology: end time issues.

The individual disciple learns and grows in faith through a greater knowledge of the substance of these essential areas. Whether you like it or not as you grow as a disciple you are engaging with theology! The level of one's engagement often determines the depth of experience and knowledge of God which is the gauge or barometer of one's spiritual growth. As a disciple it is essential for the individual to engage with theology in its various forms in order to know God in a greater and more meaningful manner. However, this will only benefit as one allows that knowledge to affect one's lifestyle; one's attitudes and actions will reflect one's grasp of theology.

Luke deals with all these theological areas in his writing; he is presenting an insight into how the embryonic church lived out its theology. As the individual disciple grows in knowledge this will firstly affect them; then those in their social context. Christianity should be summarised as a 'relational faith'. It commences with a relationship with God through Christ; continues via the relationship with Christ by the Holy Spirit; then has its outworking in relationship with others. Luke-Acts helps the reader understand how these relationships work out daily and how the local church can be a relational community. The mandate given by the Lord Jesus before his ascension was to go and make disciples this inherently means relational interaction.[7] It is impossible to communicate the gospel to someone without having contact with them; whether that is in person or over the airwaves there must be interaction. Considering how one relates to others is an essential issue in establishing one's ability to comply with the mission of God in the modern world. Luke-Acts reveals a group of people following the example of the Lord Jesus in meeting with others and meeting both spiritual and practical needs. Preaching as we will examine later is essential; biblical gospel ministry must be central in the life and praxis of the local church. However, there is also the interpersonal relationships

---

[7] Neil Hudson, *Imagine Church: Releasing Whole-Life Disciples.* (Nottingham: IVP, 2012).

that manifest themselves in many and varied ways by which the individual disciple can draw alongside others to help meet needs and live out the gospel. Paul reminds the Colossian church that it is important what we say and what we do (Colossians 3:17) as both are important in our service in the Gospel.

Chapter 2

Who, What, When and Why?
Authorship, Date and Purpose.

In as much as many have undertaken to compile a narrative of the things that have been accomplished among us... it seemed good to me also... to write an orderly account. Luke 1:1-3

As you come to study Luke-Acts there are two questions you should consider:

1. Why do you believe it necessary to study Luke-Acts?
2. What do you hope to learn from this study?

The answers to these questions will help you to focus on the purpose of study and can also be applied to every other Bible book or subject. There is a huge difference between reading and studying; we should all read the Bible systematically however, I also believe it is good to study the background to the Bible to have a better grasp on the whole story. It is not good practice to simply dive into the New Testament, without having an overview of the Old Testament and God's dealings with his chosen people Israel. Many of the principles of revelation in the OT must be understood to assist the understanding and application of NT theology.

Back to Luke-Acts! Luke-Acts is a unique piece of literature as it is written about a Jewish leader/rabbi who established a new sect which grew to become one of the world's largest religions. It was written by a non-Jew with a great interest in the spiritual aspect of Christianity and its mission in the world. It is my hypothesis that there is much one can learn from Luke-Acts that will encourage the disciple to understand how theology works out in the everyday Christian experience: affecting both the individual and the local church. I submit that Luke-Acts can be used as an outline paradigm for understanding how the embryonic church dealt with various trials, ordeals, blessings and successes. As this book progresses there are some key issues that will be discovered:

1. The unique characteristics of Lucan writing.
2. The main theological interests of Luke.
3. The centrality of Jesus in the Luke-Acts volume.
4. The opportunity to relate the full gospel to the church today.

Luke-Acts is not a manual of church practice; I do not believe there is one provided in the Bible. However, it is important for the Christian community to ask the questions raised by Gordon Fee and Douglas Stuart in relation to acceptance of issues in Acts for today. They ask:

> Are there instances from Acts of which one may appropriately say, "We must do this," or should one merely say, "We may do this"?[8]

This question should cause the individual to investigate the fuller picture of the events recorded and to assess whether they are specific to the first century cultural context. Or whether it is a specifically transferable action or further are there principles contained within the account in order to assist the modern church in its praxis. Whatever the answer to this question Acts is a document which allows the individual to assess how the early Christians adapted their knowledge of God to their context.

Contextualisation is a key issue in biblical interpretation; understanding the context of the biblical writers helps in understanding something of the writers underlying emphasis and purpose. It is important for the student to possess good quality Bible dictionary and commentaries in order to help understand the background of the biblical narrative. The helpful information gleaned from such sources will aid in the understanding of why a certain writer wrote in a style, included certain data and referred to particular people etc. Understanding and applying the principles found within the contextual situation is vital in the on-going life of the disciple. The NT is set against a context of both Jewish socio-religious-political history and pagan Greco-Roman society. Therefore, the various writers had to engage with that context and bring the divine standard to the fore. It is not enough for us to simply say we are in the 21st century and nothing else matters. The biblical context must also be taken into consideration in our desire to make the Bible appropriate to our modern cultural context. As you study the Bible be sure to research the background to the people, church or region to which a book was written; this can vastly improve your understanding

---

[8] Gordon Fee and Douglas Stuart, *How to Read the Bible for all its Worth*, (Bletchley: Scripture Union, 1994), 105-106.

and application of the biblical principles discovered. It is essential for all Christian disciples to know God in such a way that correct knowledge leads to correct action both in the Christian community and outside of that community. Understanding the overall picture of God's revelation within its context will help establish those principles that require application for a successful Christian experience.

Luke-Acts Some Background Material

Before delving into the Luke-Acts literature it is necessary to place the volume within its NT context. Traditionally this is dealt with by examining the two volumes separately; for our purposes I will take the traditional path then draw both together in order to present a common purpose.

Gospel of Luke

The Gospel of Luke is regarded as the third Gospel in the group known as the 'synoptic gospels' the others being Matthew and Mark. Each gospel writer has an emphasis as they described and assessed the life of Christ.

Syn = together

Optic = seeing

Synoptic = seeing together, viewing the same material, a blended view.

There are certain verses that illustrate the relationship between Matthew, Mark and Luke:

> Matthew 9:2-8; Mark 2:3; Luke 5:18-26;
> Matthew 10:22b; Mark 13:13a; Luke 21:17.

Biblical scholars have debated what is known as the 'synoptic problem' for many years. There are several widely accepted or suggested answers to the 'synoptic problem'. The question under consideration is how did these similarities occur?

1. Oral tradition – the historical and cultural use of oral transmission of data became so common that all gospel writers knew of the major events.
2. An early Gospel – access was gained to an early written account now lost.

3. Written fragments – some aspects of the life of Christ had been written down and used by the writers.
4. Mutual dependence – each writer drew information from the others.
5. Two major sources – Gospel of Mark (written first) & another document Quelle 'Q' = (German – source); were used by Matthew and Luke.
6. Priority of Matthew – the other 2 drew on Matthew the first document.
7. Proto-Luke; Someone possibly Luke collected unknown material into 1 document 'L' combining with 'Q' to form 'proto-Luke' he then added portions of Mark to form the third gospel.
8. Four document hypothesis – Jewish-Christian document 'M' underlies Matthew: along with Mark, 'Q' & 'L'.
9. Combination of all the above.

It is possible to accept all of these or a combination of any of the suggested paths that led to the synoptics appearing. However, all biblical investigation must rely on the ethos of 2 Timothy 3:16 which focusses on divine inspiration as the fundamental answer to the questions raised. The synoptic gospels set out a full account of the life of Christ as necessary for the framework of Christianity to be built. John's gospel with its different emphasis and style contributes to the overall picture. It is important to discover these background literary issues. However, one should not become side-tracked with them as they can detract from the purpose of engaging with Jesus and the gospel.

Material Distinctive to Luke ('L')

Luke refers to certain incidents that the other gospel writers omit. Within these areas one is confronted with some of Luke's characteristics, concerns and interests.

1. John the Baptist and Jesus: mission of John (Luke 3:1-6, 10-14, 18-20) and the genealogy of Jesus (Luke 3:23-38).
2. The rejection at Nazareth (Luke 4:16-30).
3. Certain works of Jesus: catch of fish (Luke 5:1-11), raising of widow's son (Luke 7:11-17).
4. Lessons and teachings: to disciples (Luke 9:51-56); to the seventy (Luke 10:1, 17-20); to Martha (Luke 10:38-42); about master and servants (Luke 17:7-10); ten lepers (Luke 17:11-21); and Zacchaeus (Luke 19:1-10).
5. Parables only in Luke: Good Samaritan (Luke 10:25-37); friend at midnight (Luke 11:5-8); rich fool (Luke 12:13-21); barren fig tree (Luke 13:1-9); the honoured place and hospitality (Luke 14:7-14); lost sheep,

coin, son (Luke 15); unjust steward (Luke 16:1-12); rich man and Lazarus (Luke 16:19-31); importunate widow (Luke 18:1-8); Pharisee & publican (Luke 18:9-14); pounds (Luke 19:11-27).

6. Warnings and controversies: opposition of Pharisees in Luke 11:53-14:4; Sabbath observance and woman (Luke 13:10-17); man with dropsy (Luke 14:1-6); Herod Antipas (Luke 13:31-33); and counting the cost (Luke 14:28-33).

7. Jesus' final visit to Jerusalem: approach (Luke 19:37-44); apocalyptic sayings (Luke 21:11b, 18, 25b, 26a, 28, 34-36); passion and resurrection (Luke 22:14-24).

These are areas which highlight some of Luke's personal interests; it may well be that Luke's overall purpose in writing was served by emphasising some of these areas. I will return to his purpose in writing below and examine some of these distinctives as the book develops.

The Acts of the Apostles

As Luke is traditionally treated as part of the synoptic gospels Acts is widely treated as a stand-alone volume of historical data; the general outline of its importance is considered here. The traditional view of Acts being descriptive and not prescriptive is a theory with which I contend. If we accept the gospels, which are a narrative of the life of Jesus as suitable resource for establishing theological principles, why should we not treat the narrative of Acts in the same manner? Paul's view of history as recorded in Romans 15:4 is as applicable to Acts as any other piece of biblical history:

> for whatever was written in former days was written for our instruction, that through endurance and through the encouragement of the Scriptures we might have hope.

I concur with the thoughts of Dr. D. Martyn Lloyd-Jones who deals with this issue in relation to the Holy Spirit in Acts when he writes:

> But it may well be that your position is, 'Yes, we accept that and we are in no difficulty about that. But all that ended with the Apostolic age, therefore it has nothing to do with us.' My reply is that the Scriptures are also meant to apply to us today, and that if you confine all this to the Apostolic era you are leaving very little for us at the present time. In any case how do you decide what was for them only, and what for

us also? On what grounds do you do that; what are your canons of judgement? I suggest there are none save prejudice. The whole Scripture is for us. In the New Testament we have a picture of the Church, and it is relevant to the Church at all times and in all ages.[9]

This quote from Lloyd-Jones, may be a little long, however, he does express the kernel of the issue; it being ones understanding of and acceptance of the Bible in the modern era. Is the Bible God's infallible word for all time? If the answer to this is 'yes' we do well to learn from all aspects, contexts, genres and authors who were inspired by the Holy Spirit for our learning. It is therefore imperative that we accept Acts as a biblical classroom from which the modern reader can learn theology and praxis. In Romans 15:4, Paul is referring back to the 'scriptures' that is the OT record; he contends that all the OT is there for our learning or instruction.[10] If the Christian disciple can learn from the wanderings of an embryonic nation in the wilderness or the battles of a conquering army in Joshua; how much more should we accept the historical narrative of the Spirit filled church in Acts as a rich area of teaching and learning? Those I have spoken to who hold the descriptive not prescriptive belief have all been individuals who accept the cessationist view and will not engage with the Spirit, especially tongues, as recorded in Acts 2 or the miraculous seen throughout the book. This, I suggest, is a limited view of the possibilities of how God can work through the Spirit and his people. I further submit there is a necessity to see the outworking of theology of the NT within Acts. This I believe to be Luke's key contribution to NT study i.e. allowing for a description of theology in action. How were everyday believers affected in their lives by the theology they received from the Apostles and teachers of their day? The whole of Christianity is coloured by its acceptance and application of theology. In Acts the various incidents are simply records of this theology in action. For example, in Acts 3, the healing of the man at the Temple is an illustration of the power of God to heal through the conduit of ordinary disciples; a continuation of the miraculous ministry of Jesus. At the centre of Luke's attention is the praxis of the embryonic church from which one

[9] D. Martyn Lloyd-Jones, *Preachers and Preaching* (London: Hodder and Stoughton, 1971), 314-315.

[10] F.F. Bruce, *The Books and the Parchments*, (London: Pickering, 1950); Fee & Stuart, *How to Read*, Graeme Goldsworthy, *According to Plan*, (Leicester: IVP, 2002) for an introduction to the Canon of Scripture and the commonality between the two testaments.

can glean principles that can assist the modern Christian in their understanding of church life.

Acts presents some important traditional issues by which the book can be designated a history of embryonic Christianity.

1. Message centred on the historical Jesus.
2. Age of the Holy Spirit.
3. History and development of the early Church.
4. World-wide mission.

These four areas should all be a part of the local church today; for the message must be Christ centred, Spirit empowered and spreading to unreached areas developing other Christian communities world-wide. The local church that abandons these principles will soon become spiritually dry, barren and ineffective within the context of the mission of God.[11] The Christian community must be one that is expanding and this expansion is only possible through the presence and power of the Holy Spirit glorifying Christ and introducing the gospel to the world.

Acts provides two major foci. Chapters 1-12 concentrate on the pre-Pauline experiences of the disciples in and around Jerusalem. Chapters 13-28 address the post-Pauline conversion era and Paul's immense impact on the establishing of Christian communities in the Mediterranean region. This is further summarised in assessing this book from the perspective of home mission and foreign mission, commencing in Jerusalem and culminating in Rome. It is unfortunate that Acts centres on the life of Paul; it would be of great benefit to have recorded further details of the other Apostles and their respective evangelistic ministries. I will return to the subject of mission in Part 2 below.

Another vital element of Acts is that recorded in chapter 2 and is known as the Descent of the Holy Spirit upon the new Christian community. This event ignites the Christian community setting it on a path of world-wide evangelisation and providing an example for future generations. There is a desperate need for the church to engage with the essential person and work of the Holy Spirit, it is not acceptable to engage in gospel living without the Spirit's constant presence and enabling. Acts further introduces the reader to other

---

[11] For an excellent overview of the mission of God see, Chris Wright, *The Mission of God*, (Downers Grove: IVP, 2006).

important issues in Church life; disputes, problems, leadership, miracles, power encounters; all of which are applicable to 21st century Christian communities. Gordon Fee and Douglas Stuart offer a further system by which to breakdown Acts; they offer a six-way division all of which conclude with a brief summary statement.

1. A description of the primitive church in Acts (Acts 1:1-6:7)
2. A description of the first geographical expansion (Acts 6:8-9:31)
3. A description of the first expansion to the Gentiles (Acts 9:32-12:24)
4. A description of the first geographical expansion to the Gentile world (Acts 12:25-16:5)
5. A description of the further, ever westward expansion (Acts 16:6-20)
6. A description of the events that move Paul and the gospel on to Rome (Acts 19:21-28:30).[12]

Within this hypothesis there is a useful proposal which allows the reader to see that it was God who was at work through the disciples in the forward movement of the church. This is an interesting breakdown of Acts and I submit that the issue raised about Acts being a book of movement through these various divisions is a helpful and stimulating observation. It also prompts the modern-day reader to question if they are moving forward in the gospel or have become stagnant and therefore ineffective.

When the sources of the Synoptic gospels are examined it is unusual for commentators to place Luke-Acts together; this is disappointing as one should examine the two separate volumes as one volume of Christian origins & history. I would heartily recommend Darrell Bock's publication *A Theology of Luke-Acts*.[13] as an excellent treatment of the intricacies of tying these two volumes together as a unified whole. I submit that the central issue at stake with Luke-Acts is not so much its relationship to the other gospels; rather its relationship to the NT epistles that they introduce and describe.

Luke-Acts: History and Background

As I have made clear it is essential to study Luke-Acts as a single entity in order to allow the reader the opportunity to grasp the full picture being presented by

---

[12] Fee and Stuart, *How to Read*, 98-99.
[13] Bock, *Theology of Luke-Acts*.

the author to his recipient Theophilus.

The Lukan writings consist of a gospel and a sequel there is debate over the dating of these writings. Commentators suggest a date ranging between 60 and 115 CE; Pervo suggests a date as late as 105 CE for Luke and 115 CE for Acts..[14] Whereas Donald Juel suggests placing the writings between 80-90 CE..[15] The earlier date suggested is 60-65 CE as this would allow for the exclusion of any information relating to the end of Paul's life..[16] As Peterson notes; 'A date in the 70's seems entirely reasonable… However, a good case can be made for a date as early as 62-64'.[17] This would also help explain any possible anomalies in the biblical record surrounding the writings of Timothy and Titus and a supposed visit to Spain by Paul.[18] It would further help in understanding why the author makes no reference to the writings of Paul in his account. The dating of Luke-Acts depends widely on the purpose of the writings, the author had a specific purpose in mind when he wrote and therefore if that can be ascertained then a date will more easily be discovered. My preference is for the earlier date of 62-64 CE in line with Peterson's suggestion and for the reason relating to the lack of information regarding the end of Paul's life, any discrepancies with the Pastoral Epistles and the visit to Spain not being included.

Of central importance is the person Theophilus in Luke 1:1-1 and Acts 1:1. Both works were addressed to this individual of whom more below. The author gives an excellent summary of his purpose in writing; simply to set the record straight about the life and ministry of Jesus and of his on-going work through the Church. It is possible to look at the gospel as a story about Jesus and as Acts as a book about the Holy Spirit. However, it is imperative to realise that the Spirit is only made available through the ascended Lord Jesus (John 16:7). The Spirit comes in order to enable the disciples to continue the promotion of the gospel message about Jesus in the world. Hence, I submit that Luke-Acts is all about Jesus being presented in the world and to the world. Luke-Acts allows the reader to learn lessons about engaging with a pagan world that has no thought of the truth of the gospel. The principles learned by the first disciples are relevant today for the on-going promotion of the Christian message, as the

---

[14] Pervo, *Gospel of Luke*, 6.

[15] Donald Juel, *Luke-Acts*, (London: SCM, 1984), 7.

[16] Leon Morris, *Luke*, (Leicester: IVP, 1974), 22-26.

[17] David G. Peterson, *The Acts of the Apostles*, (Apollos: Nottingham, 2009), 5.

[18] Robert Reymond, *Paul Missionary Theologian*, (Fearn: Mentor, 2000).

modern church is still challenged with gospel presentation in a world that, overall, rejects Jesus.

Luke should be considered as both a historian and a theologian; he provides a framework for examining how the early church operated in the world. I suggest, it is always beneficial to read the sections of the epistles that relate to the chronology of Acts. For example, when reading Acts 16 read Philippians; or when reading Acts 20:17-38 it is also helpful to read Ephesians, and 1 and 2 Timothy. In doing this the reader is made more aware of how the theology of Paul and the praxis of the local church dovetails to form a coherent theological foundation upon which the local church was built. With Paul's keen theological brain and Luke's emphasis on things of the Spirit and detailed historical record the two authors must be united and not divided.

Luke-Acts should then be viewed as:

1. Theologically homogeneous.
2. Luke as a theologian and historian; be careful not to dismiss Acts as purely descriptive.
3. Luke is a theologian in his own right and not simply a clone of Paul. Luke shows an interest in the essential person and work of the Holy Spirit. It is always possible for an individual to become a follower of Paul and forget that the other NT writers also contributed to the theological framework upon which the church is built. The reader does a great disservice to themselves and the church if they neglect Peter, James, John and Luke. One must always remember that ultimately the authority in the Bible rests in The Lord Jesus Christ; hence Luke's desire to record the story and teaching of Jesus.

Meeting Dr. Luke!

Who was Luke and what was his connection with the apostolic circle in the early church? The Bible gives scant information but enough to draw a sketch of his life and ministry.

1. Gentile (Colossians 4:11,14).
2. Not an eyewitness of Jesus (Luke 1:2).
3. Doctor, probably from Antioch - note then his capability for detail and intelligent records (Colossians 4:14).
4. Fellow worker in the gospel with Paul (2 Timothy 4:11).

5. One of Paul's companions, (Acts 16:4 - did he stay at Philippi or return there after leaving Paul in Rome?) and (Acts 20:6; 21:1,10,18; 27:1; 28:1,2).
6. Tradition says he died a martyr.

As a close companion of Paul, Luke would have both heard the apostolic teaching but also seen the missionary team in action. Some of the incidents referred to as the 'we passages' are those where Luke includes himself in the group are particularly interesting in assessing how theology was put into action. As Luke travelled alongside Paul et al it would allow for first-hand recording of certain key events to which the reader should pay close attention. In these incidents theology in action is key element to consider.

Luke wrote to one person: Theophilus. I will now mention a few ideas to help understand the possible identity of this character and why he was the recipient.

So, who was Theophilus?

There is considerable debate as to the identity of Theophilus. Below is a precise of what I believe to be the most likely reasons for his inclusion as the addressee of these documents.

1. An influential and well-educated Greek 'most excellent' a term of respect, who was interested in knowing more detail of the new sect known as 'Christian'.
2. A friend of Luke.
3. Theophilus could be translated as 'a lover of God' hence Luke-Acts is for all who love and serve God.
4. A man to whom this document was a defence of the Christian faith i.e. an apologetic account supporting the faith against those who wanted to see it eradicated. A possible explanation is that this was a defence document written for Paul's Roman court appearance. Such a document would have been given to the legal representatives to study pre-trial: Theophilus? This could explain why the document finishes with Paul still incarcerated under Roman jurisdiction awaiting trial. This would also help to explain the discrepancy in the timeline of Paul's life and the authorship issues that surround 1 and 2 Timothy and Titus. Furthermore, this could help explain why there is no biblical record of Paul's presumed visit to Spain following his time in Rome before re-arrest and execution. This interpretation would suggest that Luke left Paul in Rome – possibly returning to Philippi and was never able or

needed to complete the biography of the apostle. This would further support an early date for writing c.62-64 CE.

5. A Gentile believer concerned about this new sect of Jewish origins which was now being openly persecuted throughout the empire. As a result, this document would help to provide a framework for church praxis and a paradigm for facing times of adversity.

Any or none of the above could be a suitable reason for writing to Theophilus his identity is not critical in understanding Luke-Acts and it is important that the student doesn't become obsessed with such secondary issues. However, there are also some general issues that surround the purpose of writing a general history of Christian origins.

Why Write a History of Christian Origins?[19]

History is generally recorded by people with a certain purpose or agenda; often it is written by the 'victors' or the successful; hence this can give a distorted view of the facts. Luke as a thorough historian is no exception. He has a purpose; to highlight the person and work of Jesus a travelling preacher who instigated the Christian faith through his ministry. Luke wants to highlight the success of this mission. However, he is slightly different to some historians as he also records the conflicts and difficulties faced by the embryonic church. This I submit was to help the understanding of the Christian church in a twofold manner. Firstly, in order to show how Paul faced the opposition that led to his arrest and trial. Then secondly to help future generations learn from the events of the embryonic church. Luke as with the other Gospel authors has a specific aspect of the ministry of Christ in mind as he writes, he emphasises the humanity of Christ; Matthew emphasises the kingship, Mark the servant and John the divine nature. As Luke records those incidents specific to his cause he may well have had a wider purpose in writing a history of early Christianity; these could have included:

1. Construct a true history for catechetical/didactic (teaching) purposes which could be used throughout the embryonic church and for succeeding generations of disciples.

---

[19] See Peterson, *Acts of the Apostles*, 26-32 for a helpful summary of the purpose of writing.

2. Oral tradition was the standard in the ancient Jewish world – but a written record was necessary to preserve truth for succeeding generations.
3. Gentile mission saw the spread of the gospel on a wide range hence written information was necessary as apostles spread throughout the world.
4. Liturgical (worship) purposes of the early church; however as mentioned above I do not believe Luke-Acts to be a handbook for church order but simply offering guidelines and principles for the modern-day disciple to implement.
5. To support Paul in his legal battles in Rome.
6. To illustrate the issue of theology in action; how did the church react theologically and practically to the situations it faced daily.

Luke's concern is to confirm the truth of the gospel message to Theophilus and provide a new orderly narrative with accurate historical facts. The centre of his story is Jesus Christ the Lord and the on-going mission of his church. Peterson writes:

> This highly selective history is about *some* acts of *some* apostles, but more broadly about a range of people used by God to take the apostolic witness to Jews and Gentiles in various centres of the Roman Empire.[20]

As Peterson correctly indicates the story is told predominantly through the eyes of Peter, James and Paul; one wonders as to the rest of the story as seen through the eyes of the remaining apostles. Unfortunately, these records do not exist however this should not detract from the importance of the Luke-Acts narrative in charting the movement of the Gospel from a small town in Northern Galilee to the extremities of the Roman Empire and beyond. Luke centres his attention on some major divisions and then enlarges on his thinking by highlighting some key incidents. These incidents help the reader to understand more of the principle of theology in action; that which I submit is a major application of these documents.

---

[20] Peterson, *Acts of the Apostles*, 27.

Wider Purpose of Luke-Acts

Luke wrote to Theophilus as he did so he was producing a document which would provide his reader with several areas to consider further in his assessment of early Christianity. These various purposes are summarised in the eight statements below; they are general, but I believe important in building a clearer picture of the biblical narrative. Setting Luke-Acts in the wider biblical canon allows the reader to bridge the gap between the testaments providing a sense of the unity of the revelation of God in the world. These wider purposes do not include the specific issue of Luke-Acts being a legal document for use in Paul's court appearance. However, they apply to the general purpose the Holy Spirit has in providing the biblical documents for the revelation of God to humanity.

1. Transition from OT to NT.
2. The Life of Christ.
3. History and development of the early church.
4. The age of the Holy Spirit.
5. Message (kerygma) of the church centring on Jesus.
6. World-wide mission.
7. Blueprint for the church today?
8. Providing principles of/for the church in action.

Luke's intention was to produce a well-constructed historically accurate account of the life of Christ and the embryonic church; these seven areas allow the reader to follow the development of his theme. Another important issue in biblical study is to be aware of the 'big picture' that which runs from Genesis to Revelation and endeavour to set each book within that context. If one simply reads Acts with no reference to how the whole story fits together one will obtain a disjointed view of the plan of salvation. Keeping these wider purposes in mind is helpful to true understanding of the whole message running from beginning to end.

Main Divisions of Luke-Acts

1. The birth, life, ministry, death, resurrection & ascension of Jesus.
2. The Church age characterised by the Holy Spirit, mission & proclaiming Jesus.
3. Pre- Paul period: focus on Jerusalem & the embryonic church in Judea.

4. Post- Paul period focus on the expansion of Christianity to the known world through the missionary endeavours of Paul and his team.

There are some key incidents in Luke-Acts which allow the reader to follow this outline of the major divisions which join to produce a fuller picture of these pioneering years.

Key Incidents in Luke-Acts

1. Role of John Baptist as an OT prophet he is the link between OT and NT.
2. Birth of Jesus.
3. Baptism of Jesus.
4. Temptation of Jesus.
5. Ministry of Jesus.
6. Death of Jesus.
7. Resurrection of Jesus.
8. Ascension of Jesus.
9. Descent of Holy Spirit: Pentecost.
10. Early structure of Church.
11. Imprisonment of Peter.
12. Choice of deacons.
13. Martyrdom of Stephen.
14. Conversion of Saul.
15. Paul's missionary journeys.
16. Council at Jerusalem.
17. The movement of the Gospel across a continent to Europe.
18. Paul in Jerusalem.
19. Paul's journey to Rome (missionary journey no.4?).

Think it Over!

When was the last time you read the whole of Luke-Acts?

Consider spending the time reading the both documents to become familiar with their content.

Why do you want to learn more about the early church?

Do you see the need for your life and local church to be re-challenged by biblical principles found in Luke-Acts?

Chapter 3

Specific Interests: Lukan Distinctives.

In the first book, O Theophilus, I have dealt with all that Jesus began to do and teach.
Acts 1:1

Luke was an author with specific interests, that centred on Jesus, the Spirit and evangelism, and he ensured that he devoted enough space to each of these interests. His writings must not be considered as simply historical memories Luke was a man who engaged with the serious issues faced by the early church. The story of Luke-Acts unfolds from the smallest beginnings in a town in Northern Galilee to the finish in the capitol city of the Roman Empire, as he writes he builds a compelling picture of the birth of Christianity. His specific interest in the theology of the Spirit and the miraculous, especially healing, requires serious attention. Often, readers of Luke-Acts can get carried away with the spectacular records that they forget to engage with the background theology which is hugely important in providing an outline for discipleship. The following is a summary of those main areas of Lukan distinctives:

1. The Lordship of Christ (Luke 1:32; 2:11; 3:21-38; 6:5) (Acts 1:1; 2:22-36).
2. Person and work of the Holy Spirit; Luke could be labelled as theologian of the Spirit. He has an interest in the power and demonstration of the Spirit in the life of the individual; Luke-Acts is an experiential document; (Luke 1:15; 35; 41; 67; 2:25-7; 3:16, 22; 4:1) (Acts 1:5, 8; 2:1-11; 4:31; 16:6-9).
3. Prayer; (Luke 3:21; 9:18, 28-29; 11:1) (Acts 1:14; 2:42; 9:11; 10:2-4, 9; 16:13, 25).
4. Joy; (Luke 1:14,44,47; 2:10; 10:21) (Acts 8:8).
5. Peace: mentioned fourteen times in Luke and seven times in Acts, this emphasises the conflict between the Pax Romana (Roman political peace) and Pax Christi (spiritual peace of Christ) (Luke 2:14; 7:50; Acts 10:36).
6. Universal gospel; no barriers of race, creed, colour or religion, (Luke 2:14; 24:47) (Acts 2:8-11; 10:34-48).

7. Persecution; an unpopular but real theme with opposition from Jew & Roman sources. Luke emphasises the fault of the Jews in this opposition possibly as he is trying to help a Gentile convert come to terms with his faith. (Luke 2:34-5) (Acts 7).

8. Downtrodden in society; lepers/sick (remember Luke was a doctor possibly intrigued about the spiritual healing brought to these individuals), beggars, women, tax collectors, Roman soldiers, poor, (Luke 10:30-37, 38-42; 15:1-2) (Acts 4:32-37; 6:1-7).

9. Mission: The Gospel has come and must be presented in all nations Acts illustrates how the gospel begins to make inroads into 'the remotest parts of the world' (Acts 1:8). A mandate which has not been repealed.

10. Church growth: which is demonstrated by the power of the Holy Spirit in prayer, preaching, signs & wonders, cross-cultural contextualisation, and church planting.

All these above points require serious attention by the student of Luke-Acts. It may be helpful to you to take some time to look at the 10 points listed and examine how they can be applied to your life and local church situation.

Luke-Acts invites the reader to enter the praxis of the early church it could be suggested that Luke-Acts should serve as a 'blueprint' or plan for the church in succeeding generations. This may be too strong a suggestion; however, I still believe it contains serious principles that require attention in respect of how the local church community functions daily. So, how we relate the message, theology, themes and thoughts in Luke-Acts to today is of vital importance. Application of principles found in the writings will help the local church to be established in the truth & grow as a dynamic community of believers.

Issues to Address in Relation to the Theology of Luke-Acts:

All theologians will have a specific interest and even at times, over emphasise one issue above others; it is essential to note some of these issues in Luke-Acts which highlight Luke's specific emphasis.

1. Gentile inclusion in the gospel/salvation history.
2. Jewish opposition to gospel and Gentiles.
3. Mission of Christian community and growing reaction.
4. Polytheism v Monotheism: pagans/Gentiles v Christians.
5. Primitive theology of the era – remember this is embryonic Christianity!

It is important to always keep the background and context of the author/writings in mind when discovering their major theological themes as this would have affected their personal preferences for recording certain material. If Luke were writing for the specific reason of defending the faith, he would have needed to include the areas of 'conflict' between Christianity and the local religions and especially where the gospel was 'triumphant' over the accepted norm of society. This is seen for example in Acts 19:1-20 where the gospel delivered people from the local practice of magic arts and the gospel spread throughout the whole city of Ephesus.

These introductory pages have raised some issues which I hope will be clarified as this book progresses. In summary, I would submit that Luke-Acts serves as the hinge between the OT revelation of God fulfilled in the life of Christ, the emergence of the embryonic Christian Church, and the progress of the 21st century church. These two volumes of Christian origins are full of ministry, adventure, power, life and vitality, the work of a charismatic theologian which should inspire Christians today to foster the same attitude and seek to be used by God as were those in the early church. Luke is a distinctive author who sets his writings against a specific background with a specific purpose. He has areas of social, anthropological, and theological interest which shape his writing style. My intention in the rest of this book is to address these distinctive issues by way of themes to help the disciple and local church grow in the 21st century.

Does the modern-day church need to relate more to the writing of Luke-Acts? I personally believe it does and to accept the basic premise that the God who has worked can work again in a manner similar if not identically to how he has worked previously.

Think it Over!

What is your view of Luke-Acts?

Do you desire to see God work in similar ways as those recorded in the Luke-Acts narrative?

Will you seek God to reveal the truth of the need of the world and his desire and ability to 'turn the world upside down'?

Part 2
Personal Spiritual Development: Growing and Acting.

Introduction

You are witnesses to these things. Luke 24:48

In Part 2 I will set out what I believe to be the major theological themes used by Luke to support his salvation history and to bring into focus the praxis of the embryonic Christian community. These themes I have classified as 'the things that disciples and churches do in their worship and ministry.' I believe these are vital elements in the on-going progress of the 21st century church. As a result, they require some investigation and evaluation for the modern-day disciple and church to ascertain their position in God and how they relate to the biblical standards of a vital church in action.

Personal Spiritual Development: Why?

As a pastor and a teacher, I have had the important and privileged task of assisting people in their spiritual development. The sentiments of the Apostle John are so apt to describe the pastor-disciple relationship:

I have no greater joy than this, to hear of my children walking in the truth.[21]

Hence as a pastor and teacher I have a desire to see others learn and live by the biblical principles; these principles are the bedrock of one's faith and spiritual growth or development. There should be within each disciple a desire to learn more of the master – The Lord Jesus Christ – and a passion for deepening one's relationship to the Lord should characterise all true disciples. As the themes of Part 2 of this book emerge, they will make the reader aware of those principles by which the disciple should endeavour to increase knowledge which produces spirituality and action.

Part 2 will address the primary issues of:

1. Personal Spiritual Development.
2. The Church and its Operation.
3. The Church in Action.

---

[21] 3 John 4

I mentioned in the introduction that Christianity is a relational faith with its primary relationship being that between the individual and God through the Lord Jesus Christ by the Holy Spirit. The centre of discipleship and church life must be the Lord Jesus Christ; if the Christian is endeavouring to build their faith on any other foundation then disaster awaits. This is the sentiment of Jesus' teaching in Matthew 7:24-27 this popular children's Sunday school story – and song – proposes the necessity of building one's life on the rock of Christ and not the sands of time. It is interesting to note that the building may appear to be a suitable dwelling, neither builder is criticised about their structure, but the foundations are essential. In the Christian life and church things can appear ok on the outside and all appears to be well fitted together, however, when the trouble hits – the storm - then the foundations suitability is exposed. Poor foundations lead to a disaster, however, good solid foundations lead to security.

The one who focusses attention on the Lord will begin to experience spiritual growth and blessing in their everyday relationship with God. As this personal spiritual development occurs so too does the local church situation will strengthen and develop. As each part of the body is strengthened so the whole will become stronger together, Paul deals at length with this in 1 Corinthians 12-14 and we would do well to spend time investigating the principles of the body as set out in the NT. No body part can function correctly without the others and optimum capability rests in a body that is joined together with the power of Christ by the Spirit coursing through its veins. Along with the 'Spiritual Armour' of Ephesians 6 this body of Christ can be a powerful and effective force in the world for the promotion of the gospel. This principle is illustrated in Acts as the church moves forward together under the name of Christ and impacts the world.

I submit that there are three vital areas which allow for a greater spiritual growth in the life of the disciple and hence the corporate body of Christ. It must be remembered that as individuals we affect the whole; our interactions one with another can have either a positive or negative affect. One can influence others for good or bad; others in the congregation may be watching us in order to take their lead from us therefore our words, attitudes and actions can have a wide-ranging effect. If the individual concentrates upon their personal spiritual development and relationship with God, then there is a greater opportunity to show others the way forward in spiritual matters.

The three fundamental and vital areas are:

The Bible.
Prayer.
The Holy Spirit.

Throughout his writings Luke is at pains to highlight these three elements of spirituality. He does this in order to establish the credentials of the Lord Jesus and further to allow the disciple to follow their teacher into a deeper relationship. The link passage between Luke and Acts is Luke 24:44-53, here we see summarised the importance of spiritual devotion and discipleship. This is similar to Luke's introduction to Acts where he re-emphasises the centrality of spiritual devotion through the means of the word, prayer and Spirit (Acts (1:1-14). As we progress through this section of study it is essential for the individual to be honest about their personal spiritual condition. Keeping the following question in mind is helpful:

Where do I stand before God in pursuit of a greater spirituality through the word, prayer and the Spirit?

What follows is not simply an overview of Luke's desires or intentions in recording a religious history; it is a plea for all disciples and churches to respond to the basic requirements of God for a more intimate personal relationship. As John Piper puts it, we must be 'Desiring God'.[22]

---

[22] John Piper, *Desiring God*, (Colorado Springs: Multnomah Books; 1986). www.desiringgod.org

Chapter 4

Biblical Foundations: The Word of God in Luke-Acts

Were not our hearts burning within us while He was speaking to us on the road,
while He was explaining the Scriptures to us? Luke 24:32

The word of God is vital to the unfolding story of the new Christian faith without it there is no foundation upon which to build. Luke is concerned to present a true written record of God's dealing with humanity in salvation history and to record an accurate summary of the development and progress of the embryonic church. The verse above records the effect of the word on the hearts of those disciples who listened to the post-resurrection sermon from Jesus on the Emmaus Road. How deep an effect does hearing the word of God have on you as an individual? Does it cause something within to respond in a positive manner causing a 'spiritual warmth' to fill your heart? This should be the desire of both preacher and hearer, firstly that those who preach would desire to have such a positive impact and, secondly that the hearer desires that experience.

The Scriptures in Luke

What were Luke's scriptures?

Reading the word scripture in our 21st century context generally means the Bible. However, in Luke's day it referred more specifically to the OT documents. The bulk of the NT was still being written by the time Luke drew his thoughts together. Paul had penned a number of letters to various groups and although viewed as authoritative they were not yet collected into any format we know as the Bible.[23] The modern disciple has a greater advantage than Theophilus to assist in the search for true spirituality as the well-ordered and constructed collection of books we know as the Bible is freely available. Luke though relates

---

[23] See 2 Peter 3:14-18 where Peter refers to Paul's epistles and their difficult nature!

the story of salvation history to the Jewish Scriptures focussing on the fulfilment of OT prophecy in the life of Christ and of the embryonic church.

However, it is also important to point out Luke's other sources.

Word of mouth – oral tradition was key in recording the history hence Luke was dependent upon the words he heard from people who had heard from God: these may have included, Mary, Zechariah, Peter, Barnabas, Silas and Paul. During his travels and ministry, it would be appropriate to suggest that Luke, intent on discovering the truth, would have engaged with eyewitnesses (Luke. 1:2). These personal observations of the ministry of Jesus by some of his contacts would have proved invaluable. The second source would have been Luke's own personal observations and experiences. He, as we will see below, was a on a few occasions a member of the missionary team that accompanied Paul which would have added to his research base. Personal testimony is always an excellent way to pass on the message of an event. To be able to say; 'I was there' adds weight to any argument.

The central purpose of the word of God is to present a message of salvation or the mission of God, salvation history proceeds from God to mankind through the revelation of God in Christ. John reminds us that Jesus is the Logos; the revealed word of God to humanity John 1:1-14 and as such we should take notice of his words in order to establish a relationship with God Jn 14:6.

The word of God recorded in Luke-Acts can be divided into 3 main sections:

1. Period of Israel as represented in John the Baptist (Luke 1-3).
2. Ministry of Jesus (Luke 4-24).
3. The Period of the Church (Luke 24-Acts 28).

The life of Jesus and the subsequent early church is all founded upon the revealed word of God to humanity. It is imperative to remember that Luke-Acts is all about Jesus it is his life, ministry, death and resurrection that leads to his church being established his gospel being preached and his return anticipated. This encapsulates Luke's writing, his theology and themes.

We must always keep Jesus as the central person in our faith – it's all about Jesus!

The OT Fulfilled in Christ and the Church

The scriptures are important to Luke as he desires to present a picture of Jesus as the promised saviour as prophesied in the OT and as the source of enabling for the church to commence and continue to exist. The following references help to introduce the importance of the scriptures to Luke and the overall story he is portraying:

Luke 1:11-38: Revelation of the person of God and the heritage of the coming Messiah.

Luke 2:10-11,32: Revelation of the plan of salvation in fulfilment of OT prophecy.

Luke 3:4-6: Fulfilment of prophecy.

Luke 4:1-13,18-19: Defence against spiritual attack and fulfilment of prophecy.

Luke 4:18-19: Summary of the teaching of Jesus; should this be a paradigm for the 21st century church? How do we enter this ministry paradigm?

Luke 4:43: The purpose of the life and ministry of Jesus; to preach!

Luke 6:46-49: The solid foundations for life must be the word of God.

Luke 7:27: Fulfilment of prophecy.

Luke 8:4-15: The Parable of the Sower; ministry of the word, evangelism, opposition, results this is an excellent model or summary of the issues facing 21st century gospel ministry.

Luke 11:28: Focus of the ministry of Jesus and encouragement to others to follow suit.

Luke 19:38: Fulfilment of prophecy.

Luke 20:17,22: Fulfilment of prophecy.

Luke 22:22: Determined plan of God for Jesus based on the eternal decrees (word) of God.

Luke 22:37: Fulfilment of prophecy.

Luke 23:30,46: Fulfilment of prophecy.

These incidents reveal something of the width of purpose within the Word of God; it is not limited to one area of living but is vital for all aspects of Christian life. The whole of the history of Christianity is set against this background of the revelation of the Word of God to humanity. All disciples should be familiar with the whole story as presented in the biblical narrative. It is essential that an overall understanding of the 'story' is gained by all disciples, as this will enhance understanding and spiritual development.

It is a concern that some, even many, Christians limit their Bible reading to Psalms and Gospels and some of the other encouraging passages and books such as Philippians and Colossians. There is a need to read and become familiar with Genesis–Revelation, you may not understand it all but persevere and dedicate serious time to reading the OT it will serve you well and provide a framework for growth and development in the spiritual life. Luke observed the people with whom he interacted, but he was also familiar with the OT narrative to help in the presentation of the full picture of Jesus and the early Christian community.

Scriptures in Acts

Luke continues this theme in Acts where the embryonic Church is characterised as a learning Church. The promotion of the 'new faith', was left in the hands of the Apostles, these men who had spent three and a half years with the Lord were given the great responsibility of carrying on the message of the gospel.

Acts begins with the vital element of Bible teaching (Acts 1:2-4):

> 'Given orders' taught the apostles more about the kingdom of God v2.
> 'Speaking of things concerning the kingdom…' v3.
> 'Commanded…' v4, again this implies instruction.

The gospel contains more than just the way of salvation, we must preach a total gospel that firstly saves men and women, but then shows them the way to live as Christians. In Acts 20:20-27, Paul emphasises the necessity of inclusive biblical teaching in order to enhance discipleship and church growth. There are numerous church growth movements present in the 21st century however, I submit that the best model is Acts; preach the word and see people's lives changed by the power of the Spirit through the gospel. We are encouraged by Paul and Luke to proclaim the totality of biblical revelation even those parts which are not as palatable as others; this leads to a balanced diet of spiritual nutrition producing growth.

Development of the Kerygma in Luke-Acts

The kerygma or message received and proclaimed by the early church is important for Luke's purposes as he sets out his salvation history. Luke 24:36-49, provides a summary of the Lord's expectation of the apostolic preaching they were about to commence and which the 21st century church would do well to follow. I am greatly concerned about the dearth of solid biblical based, evangelical Christian preachers; for too long the Evangelical denominational Bible Colleges have been producing administrators, managers and pseudo-social workers and calling them pastors. What the church needs are pastors whose priority is to preach the word of God in a systematic expository manner in order to build up the believers.[24]. This is the main teaching of Ephesians 4:11-12, we should not get hung up on titles and positions in the church but allow individuals the ministry freedom that God has granted to them in order to equip the congregation for further ministry..[25] This has not been helped by congregations who desire to be entertained rather than challenged by the holiness of God and view the pastor as nothing more than the compere in the worship gathering who introduces the other more important people such as the song leader or worship pastor – whatever or whoever that might be! The pastor has the overall responsibility for the spiritual care of the people of God and their primary role, as with any shepherd, is to provide suitable food for growth: this comes through preaching the word regularly, faithfully, systematically and sincerely. Preaching was ordained by God for the advancement of the Christian faith and the development of the Christian disciples; let's return to the centrality of the word in the life of the pastor, Church worship and discipleship.

Luke 24:36-49 A Summary of Preaching Expectations!

Old Testament fulfilment is referred to in Luke 24:44; the NT basis for our faith is founded upon God's revelation in the OT. Commencing in Genesis 3:15 the plan of salvation is introduced and Luke records how the Christian church must continue to proclaim that same message.

Jesus uses the OT scriptures to help the disciples understand the message about himself (Luke 24:45). Modern readers often forget that when NT figures such as Jesus referred to the Scriptures, they were in fact pointing to the OT. The OT has so much to teach us especially about the Lord Jesus Christ that we do well to study it in more depth. There is much typology in the OT which refers to the future figure of Jesus the Messiah. The Book of Leviticus with its difficult to follow sacrificial system finds its fulfilment in Jesus; this is developed and more

---

[24] Vanhoozer, *Pastor as Public.*

[25] Lloyd-Jones, *Preachers and Preaching;* Stuart Olyott *Preaching Pure and Simple* (Bridgend: Bryntirion, 2005), Tim Keller, *Preaching* (London: Hodder & Stoughton, 2015).

fully explained in the NT book of Hebrews where the supremacy of Christ is taught against a backdrop of OT figures and practices.[26]

Suffering, death and resurrection (Luke 24:46): The centre of preaching must be the Lord Jesus Christ. Any message that focussing on anything other than bringing Christ and his teaching to light is ineffective. Business plans; financial well-being; social science or personal 'soapboxes' must never be the driving force of preaching; it must be Christ alone!

Repentance and forgiveness (Luke 24:47): The 21st century is a time when people are encouraged to do their own thing and accept others for what they are. Absolutes have been removed and a free-for-all spirit exists. However, when we view the world through God's eyes, we realise there is the matter of sin, another aspect dismissed by modern culture, which must be dealt with. This can only be achieved through realisation of one's condition, repentance before God and forgiveness from God. The true kerygma must contain a spiritual directive to live as God would have us live.

Witnessing (Luke 24:48): The major aspect of the second half of Acts is mission or witnessing; the divine mandate for the church is to reach out with the gospel to others. The non-witnessing church is a non-functioning church and is ineffective in the community. For the church to progress it must be a witness of Jesus.

Pneumatology (Luke 24:49): The role of the Holy Spirit is vital in the life of the believer and the corporate body of Christ. The Spirit is our source of power and ability to carry out the task given to us in this world. We ignore the Spirit at our peril. Ineffective churches are those who simply pay lip service to the Spirit and neglect his daily presence and help in their lives and ministry. Luke, a theologian of the Spirit emphasises this essential engagement with the person and work of the Spirit, I'll return to this subject below.

It is acceptable to suggest that the Apostles were simply following the pattern described to them by the risen Jesus; therefore, it is correct to state that Luke-Acts is all about Jesus and the proclamation of his gospel. In some Christian circles preaching has lost its place in the public worship of the church. This is disappointing as biblical truth must be passed on from one generation to

---

[26] F.F. Bruce, *The Epistle to the Hebrews* (Grand Rapids, MI.: Eerdmans, 1990), Stuart Olyott, *I Wish Someone would Explain Hebrews to Me* (Edinburgh: Banner of Truth, 2010).

another and this is possible through the 'foolishness of preaching'. If the 21st century church is to be strong and make an impact it must have solid biblical foundations which are available through the preached word. There is a desperate need within the 21st century evangelical church for a return to biblical based preaching this is the divine standard for introducing people to the message of the gospel. The Apostolic paradigm of preaching the word of God should be accepted today as the primary divine means for communicating Christ to the world.

Speeches in Acts

The sermons or public speeches in Acts relate to the theological content of the embryonic church. It developed in the following manner:[27]

1. Age of fulfilment has dawned OT promises come to fruition in Jesus.
2. Jesus is:
   a) descended of David,
   b) travelled, taught, produced mighty works, by power of God,
   c) crucified in God's plan,
   d) raised by the power of God.
3. The Church is witness to these things.
4. Jesus has been exalted and now reigns as the Messianic head of the 'New Israel'.
5. The Holy Spirit is in the Church as Christ's presence and power.
6. Jesus will come again for judgement and restoration of all things.
7. All who hear message should repent and be baptised.

The speeches/sermons record the context of events as they occurred illustrating how people reacted to certain situations. The speeches are recorded in Acts 1:15-26; Acts 2:14-40; Acts 3:11-4:20; Acts 5:29-32; 7; Acts 8:32-40; Acts 10:34-48; Acts 13:16-43; Acts 17:16-32; Acts 20:17-35; Acts 22-24; Acts 26; Acts 28:17-32. These serve as an excellent source of primitive theology.

The key theological themes that can be found in these speeches are:

Crucifixion
Resurrection
Salvation

---

[27] F.F. Bruce, *The Speeches in Acts*, (London: Tyndale, 1942).

Repentance

Use of OT

Missiology (witness/evangelism)

Judgement

Pneumatology

The sermons are important because within them it is possible to trace an early if somewhat primitive theology especially Christology and pneumatology, two of Luke's prominent themes. It is a good discipline to read the sermons in Acts and discover this early theology and then marry this to the more developed thinking of Paul in his epistles where he interprets the theology in accordance with every day Christian life. These themes are essential to the on-going development of the Christian community. Their presentation in sermons, teaching and preaching will be an excellent barometer as to the health of the local church and to the spiritual depth of both leaders and congregations. It is vital that the 21st century church continues to preach the gospel in its full orbed glory and expected power. Much of the power of God appears to be latent in recent years as the church focusses on programmes and management style to the detriment of preaching the truth of the gospel. The divine paradigm for preaching remains in place for the benefit of the local church and wider community..[28]

A central theme of Luke-Acts is the Word of God which reveals:

1. Divine plan (Luke 22:22).
2. Risen Lord Luke 24:1-12; Acts 2:22-24; Acts 17:31-2).
3. Kingdom of God (Acts 1:2-3).
4. Name of Jesus (Luke 1:31-33; Acts 4:12).
5. Repentance and faith (Acts 2:380.
6. Suffering of the Lord and Church (Luke 23:11-49; Acts 4:3; 5:18).

F.F. Bruce comments that:

> This teaching was authoritative because it was the teaching of the Lord communicated through the Apostles in the power of the Spirit..[29]

---

[28] Stuart Olyott, *Preaching Pure and Simple,* (Bridgend: Bryntirion Press, 2005); John Piper, *The Supremacy of God in Preaching,* (Grand Rapids: Baker, 1990/2004). Vanhoozer, *Hearers and Doers*. Vanhoozer, *The Pastor*.

[29] F.F. Bruce, *Acts,* 73.

This should be the desire of every preacher in the any era to be authoritative and Spirit empowered; anything else is simply not preaching! The learning process should never end for the Christian, there is so much to know about God, contained in his word, that we should never run out of material for learning. This understanding is supported by Paul when he writes to Timothy about development of the individual in the things of God (2 Timothy 3:16-17) and to the Ephesians (Ephesians 4:11-12). Discipleship is an on-going process of growth and development as such the Christian disciple should engage with the means available from God to sustain growth; the primary means is the Word of God. It is important to note that the Apostles received instruction about the Spirit before his arrival and not vice versa. To underestimate the position of constructive and instructive teaching and overemphasise the Spirit in Acts is to do a disservice to the Christian community. No one saw the arrival of the Spirit as the end of biblical teaching and as the time to dispense with human teachers, but as Stott comments, the new converts: 'sat at the Apostles' feet, hungry to receive instruction, and they persevered in it.'.[30] Biblical teaching can never be replaced by any other form or aspect of worship; the word of God remains the bedrock for the faith. Howard Clark Kee comments:

> Throughout Acts, the proclamation of the word is a central concern and the major factor in the spread of the new community. It is in response to the word heard and believed that the group continued to grow by the thousands in Jerusalem..[31]

The matter of educating disciples and preaching to the masses was a focal point of the Early Church. It was, and remains, imperative for a balance to exist between true biblical knowledge and the interpretative work of the Spirit (John 16:15-16). Submission to the NT paradigm of Spirit inspired biblical instruction is essential for the 21st century Christian community. The Bible should never be relegated to the position of an 'also ran' in the life of the Christian but should be relied upon for a balanced life and experience. I offer a plea to all pastors and leaders restore the preaching of the word to a central role in your corporate worship; allow the word of God to penetrate the hearts of people but first it must penetrate your heart and mind. The leader who neglects the word of God on a

---

[30] Stott, *Message of Acts*, 82.
[31] Howard Clark Kee, *Good News to the Ends of the Earth*, (London: SCM, 1990), 72.

personal level and then further neglects it on a corporate level is destined for spiritual disaster.

Think it Over!

Why is it important to have a solid foundation in the Christian life?

What role does teaching/learning play in your Christian life?

Do you spend time looking at God's word and asking Him to lead you into the truth?

Do you regularly attend preaching services where the word of God is expounded and explained?

Chapter 5

It's Good to Talk: Prayer in the Church

And He said to them, 'when you pray say: Father hallowed be your name'. Luke 11:2

Prayer in Luke's Gospel

Prayer is our primary source of communication with God, Luke 11:1-12. Notice it says in verse 2, *'when you pray'*, not 'if you pray.' Prayer then is no optional extra for the true disciple of Jesus. John Piper makes some excellent points on the necessity of prayer he writes:

> Life is war. That's not all it is. But it always is that. Our weakness in prayer is owing largely to our neglect of this truth. Prayer in primarily a wartime walkie-talkie for the mission of the church as it advances against the powers of darkness and unbelief..[32]

Piper is correct in that many disciples of Jesus focus on the benefits of a 'father figure' who is there for one's blessing and for providing good things. However, often forgetting that the Christian life is first and foremost a spiritual battle being played out in the heavenly realms between God and the Devil; and the disciple is right in the middle of the conflict and requires constant communication, battle plans and support from their heavenly Father. It is a great sadness to hear of local churches and individuals who neglect the prayer meeting, there is a desperate need for the church to re-engage with the issue of prayer both corporate and individual: it is time to return to prayer as that vital element of true Christianity.

Often the disciple can adopt a very haphazard attitude to prayer however the Lord emphasises this vital avenue of discipleship and is emphasised by

---

[32] John Piper, *Let the Nations Be Glad*, (Nottingham: IVP, 1993/2003) 45, see Piper's chapter 2 'The Supremacy of God in Missions through Prayer' 45-69 for some great insights into the necessity of prayer in discipleship and mission.

following the example of Jesus throughout his life and ministry (Luke 5:16; 6:12; 9:18; 11:1; 18:1).

1. Prayer was an accepted part of Jewish worship and occurred 3 times daily, 9am (Acts 2:15), 12 noon (Acts 10:9), 3pm (Acts 3:1).
2. Prayer was both public and private (Luke 18:9-14; Acts 10:9).
3. Prayer is a source of praise, thanksgiving, adoration, intercession.
4. Prayer was generally performed standing, or kneeling and bowing the head, generally, hands were lifted.
5. Prerequisites of prayer; sincerity, repentance, consecration, faith, submission to will of God, (Luke 18:9-14 a true attitude in prayer).
6. Christ prayed; (Luke 5:16; 6:12; 9:18; 11:10).
7. Disciples encouraged to pray; (Luke 11:2-13; 22:40 help in temptation).
8. We are encouraged to pray; (Luke 18:1-17).

Prayer in Acts

From the time of the Ascension, the small community engaged itself in one aspect of worship, which was an area of their lives encouraged by the Lord – prayer. (Acts 1:14 *'devoting themselves to prayer'*). Prayer was not a passing fad but an expectant anticipation of the promised Spirit, therefore they were persistent and committed to this act of worship (Acts 2:42). Today it is essential that the Christian community be a praying one; prayer is the divine standard of communication throughout the biblical narrative and remains as such today. Notice they had to pray even though the Lord had promised, his promises do not render praying irrelevant, in fact they should cause us to pray more as we seek God's blessing. Stott commenting on the necessity of prayer states:

> We learn, therefore, that God's promises do not render prayer superfluous. On the contrary, it is only his promises which give us the warrant to pray and the confidence that he will hear and answer.[33]

Throughout the Acts record we are confronted with a praying church the following list provides an outline of the importance of prayer and its many faceted purpose.

1. Mattias is chosen after praying (Acts 1:24).
2. the Spirit arrives after prayer (Acts 1:14; Acts 2:1).

---

[33] Stott, *Acts*, 54.

3. Prayer is vital ingredient in church life (Acts 2:42).
4. The lame man is healed after prayer (Acts 3:1-6).
5. Peter and John are released from prison after prayer (Acts 4:24, 31).
6. Forgiveness is seen as available by the means of prayer (Acts 8:22-24).
7. Deliverance through prayer (beware doubt) (Acts 12:5).
8. Mission preceded by prayer (Acts 13:2-3).

Important incidents in the life of the embryonic church are covered in prayer; the apostles and the rest of the disciples brought themselves together in order to pray. It was C.H. Spurgeon who said, 'I should rather teach one man to pray then ten to preach'; this sentiment from the Prince of Preachers is one we should revisit in the 21st century. Too many people are looking for the answer to public ministry how can we attract people to the Gospel? How can I be a better communicator? Spurgeon's answer is simple: pray! And what an impact his ministry made in 19th century Britain. If the Christian is always at prayer, then there is hope for their spiritual growth and the further impact of the gospel within their wider sphere of influence.

'Lord teach us to pray' is probably one of the greatest requests ever made by the disciples and we too should echo that request. It is good practice for the Christian to read Christian biography if you desire to see how God can work through prayer seek out the story of George Muller a man who proved the necessity of prayer in order to feed hundreds of children in Bristol.[34] Prayer is an integral aspect of the Christin experience which is supported throughout the writings of the NT. Without prayer the individual loses the direct contact with God that is necessary in order to direct our ministry for him (Matthew 6:5-15).

Paul further deals with prayer in 1 Timothy 2:1-8. The urgent call to prayer for the Christian and especially the pastor: 'exhort' carries the weight of meaning as to urge or call upon individuals to engage with prayer. The apostle is concerned that Timothy pays serious attention to this subject. No one can afford to neglect the avenue of prayer; whoever we are, whatever we may know, we cannot progress without the essential ministry of prayer.

What is prayer? The area of prayer can be divided into four basic categories:

Supplications/entreaties: precise requests or specific needs.
Prayers: general term for confessions/adorations.

---

[34] Roger Steer, *George Muller: Delighted in God,* (Fearn: Christian Focus, 2015).

Petitions/intercessions: prayer on behalf of others

Thanksgivings: prayers of praise

Why Pray?

I suggest a threefold purpose:

1. It is for personal benefit; growth, direction and help (Matthew 6:6; Matthew 7:7-12).
2. It is for the benefit of others (Ephesians 1:15-18; Ephesians 3:14-21).
3. To align the minds of the supplicant with the will of God for their situation. This is often overlooked by the supplicant, as prayer is made remember that it is as much an opportunity for God to change their minds and align them with his will and purposes as it is to get God to think and act as they desire!

If the individual approaches prayer with these three purposes in mind, then it will help to move the act of prayer away from a 'shopping list' approach of requests to a place where God's true will is being discovered.

Paul speaks much about prayer in his epistles and here we see a necessity of balance in our prayers; the Bible is a book of balance and we must not over-emphasise one aspect to the detriment of another. Never get carried away with one teaching but be a student of the whole of the Bible doctrine and tradition (Acts 20:20).

Prayer references in Paul's writings help the disciple to understand further why prayer is necessary: Philippians 4:6-7; Colossians 1:3, 4:2-6; Ephesians 1:15-23, 6:18-19; 1 Thessalonians 5:17. Paul's thinking is summarised in 1 Timothy 2:1-5.

Reasons for Prayer as Suggested by Paul in 1 Timothy 2:1-5.

v2 - social and political peace in order that Christians can live out their faith.

v2 - provides dignity for the soul.

v3 - provides salvation for others.

v4 - allows us to participate in the heart desire of God.

v5 - there is a mediator for us to come to God and that is Jesus; he is the point of contact between humanity and the Father in order that we can participate in the on-going work of the gospel. (Hebrews 7:25).

If the disciple of Christ desires to move forward in their faith, to grow to maturity in Christ, to experience a greater blessing of God in their life then they must pray. Prayer can be one of the hardest disciplines in life; it requires time, commitment and desire. It is good practice to make a prayer list that can guide you through your prayer time, often when we have no focus in our prayers we can wander and become ineffective. It is good to have times of silent waiting on God; prayer is a two-way thing wait in the presence of God for the direction and answers you are seeking. Too much talking can prevent the word of God speaking into your situation.

Luke encourages the Disciples of Christ to pray by the very fact that he records many incidents of prayer within the Christian community.[35]

Think it Over!

Do you pray?

Why do you pray?

Does prayer change things?

Who is changed, God or us?

---

[35] For further discussion on prayer see: Grudem, *Systematic Theology*, 376-396; A.A. Hodge, *Evangelical Theology*, (Edinburgh: Banner of Truth, 1990), 84-96; Dennis L. Okholm, 'Prayer', in Walter A. Elwell (Ed.), *The Evangelical Dictionary of Biblical Theology*, (Grand Rapids: Baker, 1996), 621-626.

Chapter 6

I Can't Cope Alone: The Holy Spirit Power for Service

But you will receive power when the Holy Spirit comes on you to be my witnesses.
Acts 1:8

Luke could be viewed as the theologian and historian of the Spirit he has an acute interest in the power of the Spirit in the life of the embryonic Christian community. The Spirit dominates his thinking and writing from his first chapter. The Spirit is very much viewed as the eschatological Spirit and places the whole story of the embryonic church in the 'last days.' As a result, this emphasis allows Luke to focus on the necessity of spiritual power in order to fulfil the Great Commission to preach the gospel or be witness and speak about the KOG. As G.B. Caird comments:

> The Holy Spirit in the Bible is always the imminent power of the Living God, who through human agency is shaping history to his own ends; and in the New Testament the Spirit is always the gift of Christ, whereby men are enabled to participate in his ministry and purpose.[36]

Darrell Bock commenting on the Spirit states: 'His key role is as the sign of the new era, the giver of life that enables and directs the community.'[37] I concur with Bock and submit the 21st century Christian must pay greater attention to the vital person and work of the Spirit. I once saw a comment on Facebook made by the late Reinhard Bonnke: 'The less Holy Spirit we have the more coffee and cake we need to keep the church going'. It is so true that more time is spent debating the type of coffee and the time it is served on a Sunday than is spent seeking God to visit his people by the Spirit as they gather for corporate worship! The life of the disciple of Jesus must be one dominated by the Spirit. This is not to say all Christians should be running around giving so called

---

[36] G.B. Caird, *The Apostolic Age*, (London: Duckworth, 1962), 57; John Michael Penney, *The Missionary Emphasis of Lukan Pneumatology*, (Sheffield: Sheffield Academic Press, 1997).
[37] Bock, *Acts*,

'prophetic words' to everyone or performing great miracles but allowing the Spirit to guide, comfort, instruct, lead and when necessary demonstrate his power through his people. The role of the Spirit is vast and unfortunately the Christian church has either over-emphasised the spectacular or ignored the basic necessity of the Spirit's presence and thereby both sides have become ineffective extremes of teaching. I return to one of my 'pet subjects' balance in all things spiritual and a serious study of the biblical role of the Spirit will lead to healthier Christian lifestyles and a more vibrant, evangelistic and powerful church.

Before proceeding with this chapter simply stop and consider:

1. Are you aware of the Holy Spirit?
2. What do you understand of the Spirit's role?
3. Are you open to teaching on the Spirit?
4. What difference can the Spirit make in your experience?

The Spirit is a part of all the synoptic gospels however Luke pays much closer attention to his essential work.

References to the Spirit in the Synoptic Gospels[38]

Mark	Matthew	Luke
1:8	1:18-20	1:15
1:10	3:11	1:17
1:12	3:16	1:35
3:29	4:1	1:41
12:36	10:20	1:67
13:11	12:18	2:25-7
	12:28	3:16
	12:31-32	3:22

---

[38] Roger Stronstad, *The Charismatic Theology of Saint Luke*, (Peabody: Hendrickson, 1984), 35.

Mark	Matthew	Luke
	22:43	4:1
	28:19	4:1
		4:14
		10:21
		11:13
		12:10
		12:12

The Spirit in Luke

The Spirit is viewed in several ways:

1. Life giving (Luke 1:35).
2. Inspirational (Luke 1:41-42).
3. Directive (Luke 2:27).
4. Experiential (Luke 3:16).
5. Infilling (Luke 4:1).
6. Empowering (Luke 4:18).

Luke highlights the transfer of the person of the Spirit from OT individuals at special times and for special purposes e.g. OT prophets, Elizabeth, Mary, Simeon, to the community in general as in Acts 2:1-11. The Spirit was now a personal experience available to all individuals.

Acts 2:39 is a vital text in ones understanding of the personal work of the Spirit upon the individual; this text is key for many Pentecostal/Charismatic theologies. Jesus commenced a charismatic ministry (Luke 3:16,22; Luke 4:18) and he is seen as the bearer and giver of the Holy Spirit (Luke 24:49; Acts 1:5-8; John 16:7).

This experiential Spirit is available today and should be engaged with in a greater dimension than is currently so in the local church. It is the Spirit who can bring the freedom, liberty, conviction and blessings required. Congregations do not need to be whipped up by human agencies but open up to the all-powerful Spirit. As lives are opened, so they will be radically changed and charged with the raw power of God. Luke records much of this raw power in action; the norm for a supernatural charismatic church.

The Spirit in Acts

The pivotal event of the Book of Acts is recorded in chapter 2; the arrival of the Holy Spirit into the new community of believers. This supernatural outpouring opened the way for the establishment of the New Testament Church.

The person and work of the Holy Spirit is a vast subject, and needs a deeper investigation, there are many books and papers available on the subject and the serious student should endeavour to read as many as possible in their pursuit of the knowledge of God.[39] One thing we can state with certainty is that the person and work of the Spirit is essential in the Christian experience and a greater understanding of this spiritual blessing is necessary if we are to grow both spiritually and numerically.

Spiritual power is of interest to Luke, as a Doctor of Medicine, he is also interested in how the spiritual power affects physical recovery in individuals of which more later as I engage with the miraculous. However, Luke's primary concern with the Spirit is his enabling power to allow for a greater expansion of the gospel. Christians are to be witnesses of the Lord Jesus and this witness must be charismatic in its emphasis without the Spirit the individual cannot succeed in the ministry of the word, the presentation of the gospel and the salvation of souls becomes impossible.

> Acts 1:2 - means of understanding God's commands.
> Acts 1:5 - spiritual baptism experiencing an emersion in the Spirt.
> Acts 1:8 - spiritual empowerment or enabling for witnessing; this is the key issue that led to the formation of Pentecostal doctrine and praxis in the early 20th century. The question which has been widely debated is 'is there any physical evidence which proves an individual has received the Spirit?'
> Acts 2:4 - Spirit inspired utterances/languages unlearned by the speaker but known by hearers.

---

[39] Keith Warrington, *The Message of the Holy Spirit,* (Nottingham: IVP, 2009); J.I. Packer, *Keep In Step With The Spirit,* (Leicester: IVP, 1984, 2005).

Acts 2:14-39 - the result of spiritual power a penetrating evangelistic sermon; this is often overlooked by teachings that focus on other aspects of Acts 2. The Spirit came in order to enhance witnessing. I submit it is necessary for the 21st century church to revisit this teaching and seek God's power for service and not to be focussed on spectacular revelatory gifts or the miraculous.

Acts 4:8 - *'filled with the Spirit'* a Lukan term which emphasises the complete reliance of the individual upon the Spirit.

Acts 4:31 - a demonstration of the Spirit's power through physical manifestations. Let us not limit God to human preconceived ideas of how God should work. The Spirit can and does work outside of the natural human realm in order to draw attention to the Lord Jesus.

Acts 5:3 - illustrates the personality of the Spirit; he can be lied to as a result we must be very careful as to what we say and how we live.

Acts 6:3, 5 - Visible, knowable, experiential, and experimental? How do we know someone is 'full of the Spirit' as these men in Acts 6 were recognised?

Acts 7:51 - the Spirit can be resisted that is individuals can turn themselves away from the Spirit's work and calling hence rejecting God's will and purpose.

Acts 7:55 - *'full of the Holy Spirit'*.

Acts 8:15, 17 - reception of the Holy Spirit post conversion.

Acts 8:18-19 - impartation of the Spirit through laying on of hands 2 Tim 1:6 which is generally accepted as being the accepted manner of bestowing blessing upon another.

Acts 8:29 - direction comes from the Spirit.

Acts 8:39 - power of the Spirit demonstrated.

Acts 9:17 - reception of the Spirit by laying on of hands with the immediate effect of healing.

Acts 10:19-20 - direction and revelation comes via the Spirit.

Acts 10:44 - direction and revelation from the Spirit.

Acts 11:16 - Spirit and the word must never be separated.

Acts 11:24 - *'full of the Holy Spirit'*. How was this recognised?

Acts 11:28 - revelation of the divine plan.

Acts 13:2 - revelation of future events.

Acts 13:4 - Spirit is the instigator of mission.

Acts 13:9 - *'full of the Spirit'*.

Acts 13:52 - *'filled with the Spirit'*.

Acts 16:6-7 - negative direction of the Spirit. It is important for the reader to understand that sometimes God says 'no' through the Spirit; how one reacts to that situation can be a true measure of one's spirituality.

Acts 19:2 - Spirit received post-salvation.

Acts 19:6 - reception of the Spirit led to tongues and prophecy; should there be accompanying signs of the Spirit's arrival?

Acts 19:21 - Spirit's guidance and direction.

Acts 20:23 - revelation of the Spirit.

Acts 20:28 - Spirit provides leaders in the church.

Acts 21:11 - revelatory and confirmatory ministry of the Spirit.

Acts 28:25 - inspiration of the word of God.

With this amount of references to the Spirit in Acts we can state with certainty that:

1. Luke had a major interest in the work of the Spirit.
2. The Spirit is essential to Christian discipleship.
3. 21st century Christians who neglect the Spirit do so at their spiritual peril.

Luke and the Spirit: A Summary.

1. Fulfilment of the words of Jesus (Luke 24:49).
2. The Spirit is the believer's source of power for witnessing. The fulfilment of the Old Testament prophets (Acts 2:16).
3. The provision of God for the church to function (Acts 1:8).
4. Filled with the Spirit is a specific Lukan term – emphasising the totality of spiritual experience. The term Spirit baptism has become more widely used since the emergence of the Pentecostal movement in the early 20th century. This terminology has led to wide ranging debate within evangelical circles however, the emphasis, whatever one's doctrinal position, is to know a full experience of the Spirit in one's life.[40]

---

[40] For more information on the emergence of the Pentecostal movement see; Walter J. Hollenweger, *The Pentecostals,* (London: SCM Press, 1972); Cecil M. Robeck, Jr. *The Azusa Street Mission & Revival,* (Nashville, TN: Thomas Nelson, 2006); Palmer, *The Emergence of Pentecostalism.*

5. Through the Spirit the presence and power of Jesus are known in the church.
6. Christianity develops through the power of the Spirit.
7. The prominence of the power of God through the Spirit enables a 'fringe' community struggling with acceptance to make a mark in society.
8. The Spirit is an eschatological sign (Acts 2:16-21).

Take the opportunity to read Acts 1-2 and think about your understanding of the personal importance of the Holy Spirit in your life and experience. The essential person and work of the Spirit can be neglected by some individuals due to a fear of excess in the spiritual realm. This is possible if we over emphasise one aspect of the Spirit's work above another hence balance in our teaching and praxis is vital. As a result of this and in order to gain a balanced perspective it is essential that the individual studies all aspects of the Spirit's work and does not simply focus on the Acts 2. It is good practice to read the Lord Jesus' words on the role of the Spirit in John 14-16. and with the epistles where we can engage with a fuller picture of the pneumatological teachings. An engagement with the Spirit will produce a more vibrant and effective individual disciple, local church and world mission for the Spirit comes to make known the work of Jesus in the world.

Why Do We Need the Spirit Today?

This is an essential question as disciples endeavour to 'Act Out Their Christianity' for this is only truly effective when the Spirit empowers, enables, guides, directs and grows the individual. The disciple is encouraged in Luke 11:13 to ask for the Spirit because this will enhance their effectiveness in the gospel ministry. Luke records the necessity of continually asking, seeking and knocking that is having a persistent attitude towards the spiritual desires to be fulfilled in one's life and experience (Luke 11:5-12). Luke insists that whatever good gifts the disciple receives all come from God the father who desires the best for his children; and what better gift is there than the Holy Spirit, who dwells within for one's good. As Luke records the necessity to engage with the Spirit and highlights in Acts how the Spirit influences the individual and church, other NT writers also emphasise this critical issue. Engaging with the Spirit is not a theological position that belongs solely to the Pentecostal movement, all Christians should experience the fullness of the Spirit. It is worth remembering that there were no denominations in the NT simply Spirit filled believers preaching the gospel. Is this a model to which the 21st century church should return? I suggest; yes! Is it time to move away from narrow denominational lines and seek fellowship with Bible believing Christians, who desire a vital and active relationship with the Lord through the Holy Spirit? If the NT Church functioned as it did with great success (not a word to be avoided in spiritual matters) then why shouldn't we return to that pneumatological empowered faith and witness the Word of God grow beyond our greatest imaginations (Ephesians 3:20).

John and Paul along with Luke, contribute greatly to the discussion on the Spirit in the life of the disciple.

Acts 1:8 is of course the Pentecostal focus of Spirit baptism, the power to witness is essential. The disciple cannot enter the spiritual realm without the ever-present Spirit. Trying to witness in one's own strength is ineffective the Spirit is provided for the disciples enabling and should not be neglected. This is a major aspect of Luke-Acts, which I will return to below as I consider Mission in Acts. Is your witness effective? If not, can I suggest it may be because you are relying on self rather than the Spirit.

In Romans 8:16 Paul reminds his readers, and us, of the vital role the Spirit plays in bringing the assurance of salvation. As N.T. Wright states:

> When the holy spirit comes to dwell in a person's heart, the first sign is that they recognize God as father; this, I think, is part of what Paul meant in 5:5 (Romans) when he spoke of a love for God being poured out in our hearts by the holy spirit. The cry 'Abba father' uses the old Aramaic word which Jesus himself had used for God (Mark 14.36).[41]

Wright's sentiments are correct and encouraging, for what a great work of the Spirit; bringing that wonderful assurance of an intimate relationship with the father is, especially at those low points in one's experience; it is always good to rely on the Spirit's help and not human emotion.

Paul continues to highlight the Spirit's vital role in Rom 8:26. Here the Spirit comes to the assistance of the troubled but praying disciple. There can come times in the disciple's prayer life that you simply don't know what to pray or how to pray the Spirit steps in or as Moo translates; 'comes to the aid of', 'joining

---

[41] N. T. Wright. *Paul for Everyone Romans Part 1: Chapters 1-8* (London: SPCK, 2004) 146.

with to help', 'bearing a burden along with.' [42] Moo comments further that the Spirit, 'joins with us in bearing the burdens imposed by our weakness.' Often as humans we are unaware of how to pray correctly, it is at those times that the Spirit intervenes and takes our deepest heart felt longings to the father through the son. It's comforting to know that when things get tough the Spirit is in control.

Spiritual gifts and their operation have been a subject of much contention for many years especially since the arrival of the Pentecostal movement in the early 20th century.[43] However, it is important not to get lost in the debates on cessationism and lose sight of the fat that the Lord can work as he wills in people's lives. This is the point Paul makes in 1 Corinthians 12:1-11 where the Spirit distributes gifts as he wills and not as we will or wish. If you are someone who struggles with the whole charismatic question, I simply ask you to consider whether the Lord can work in such a 'pentecostal' manner and help the individual and church in their mission and spiritual growth. All I would say is be careful not to accept some aspects of Paul's teaching in 1 Corinthians and ignore others because they don't fit with your view of what is proper for Christian behaviour.

John 14-16 are chapters that are essential to the understanding of the Spirit's work. Here the apostle engages with the thoughts and words of the Lord Jesus in a few important texts. John 14:16 the Spirit is our ever-present helper, the comforter or advocate, the one who draws alongside to help. John 14:26 and John 16;13 introduces us to the Spirit our teacher the one who guides the disciple in the truth. How essential it is that all disciples know the truth of the Lord and the Gospel as revealed in the biblical narrative. If you are struggling to understand the Bible seek the Spirit's help, he will guide your understanding. The role of the Spirit is further explored in John 16:8 where we encounter his role in mission and evangelism. One vital role is that of convicting and convincing men and women of sin, righteousness and judgement. Why is this so important? Because this is a task we cannot achieve in our own strength or by our own abilities or cleverness. The whole issue of salvation is a spiritual undertaking and the Spirit must be employed in seeing people come to a true

---

[42] Douglas Moo. *The Epistle to the Romans*, NICNT, (Grand Rapids/Cambridge: Eerdmans, 1996) 523.

[43] William Kay. *The Pentecostals in Britain* (Carlisle: Paternoster, 2000). Palmer, *Emergence.* Cecil M. Robeck Jr. *The Azusa Street Mission and Revival* (Nashville: Thomas Nelson, 2006.

knowledge of God. The role of the disciple is to seek God to work on people's hearts by the Spirit and prepare the way for the simple words we preach to impact with power. Finally, John tells his readers that the Spirit simply wants to glorify Jesus Jn 16:14. The Spirit is not set on promoting self or people, however great a preacher they may be, he is set solely on glorifying Jesus. What this world needs is a church that through the power of the Spirit glorifies the Lord Jesus Christ. For if he is truly glorified others will come to know him, love him and serve him.

Paul continues to explain the role of the Spirit in the disciple's life in Galatians 5:22-23, a passage relating to the production of spiritual fruit in one's life. In Galatians 5:1-25 Paul emphasises the necessity of walking or living in or by the Spirit, and as a result of having this spiritual nature, planted by the Spirit in us, the correct fruit or outcomes in character are produced. Love, joy, peace, patience, kindness, goodness, faithfulness, gentleness, self-control, and who does not need all of these attributes in their life?

The role of the Spirit is essential and a vast subject, here I have engaged with what I submit are the salient texts which give a general overview of the essential person and work of the Spirit. This is one area of study I would suggest all disciples need to engage with in a greater manner, there are numerous books available on the Spirit, take some time to invest in a few to help your understanding of his vital ministry.[44]

Think it Over

How do you see the role of the Holy Spirit in the life of the believer?

Should the 21st century church be a 'charismatic' entity?

Are you open to the Spirit's moving in your life?

Conclusion

In this section I have examined the place of the word, prayer and the Spirit suggesting that they are the three fundamental building blocks of Christian discipleship and are central to the church. As you contemplate your personal

---

[44] Fredrick Dale Bruner. *A Theology of the Holy Spirit* (Grand Rapids: Eerdmans, 1970). Packer. *Keep in Step*. Clark H. Pinnock *Flame of Love: A Theology of the Holy Spirit* (Downers Grove: IVP, 1996).

situation and that of your local Christian community take some time to examine where you stand in relation to these three vital elements. I submit that any individual or corporate body of Christ which desires to make progress must engage with these three, divine means of growth and sustenance. If the aim is to be an active Christian there must be a solid foundation upon which one can act, according to Luke-Acts this foundation is word, prayer and Spirit. As we move into the next section of this book, we will examine how the Christian community based on these three spiritual principles operates to its optimum.

Part 2A

The Church and its Operation

Introduction

Now the multitude of those who believed were of one heart and one soul; neither did anyone say that any of the things he possessed was his own, but they had all things in common. Acts 4:32

As the individual develops a personal Christian identity through spiritual disciplines, they must be careful not to think that the Word, Spirit and prayer are the only issues that require attention. Some disciples can get trapped in a 'super spiritual' outlook that results in them dwelling on the ethereal and supernatural and forgetting the impact faith should have on their everyday living and actions. The spiritual disciplines of word, Spirit and prayer, as mentioned in the previous chapters, are the main means of grace by which the individual grows or develops a deeper spirituality.[45].

In the next few chapters I will suggest five further essential areas that relate to one's spirituality and the operation of the Christian community. These five areas are: unity, fellowship, breaking of bread, water baptism and church organisation. These are areas that every disciple must be aware of and understand their centrality in the on-going effective operation of the local Christian community.

As the individual endeavours to act out their Christianity these issues are paramount in presenting a biblically based picture of what it is to be a true disciple of Jesus. All the practices the disciple of Christ is involved in must have a positive effect on other disciples and the wider community. This effectiveness will be enhanced by a greater understanding of the basic principles set out in the following chapters.

---

[45]'Means of Grace' refers to those things freely provided by the grace of God for the spiritual benefit of the individual generally accepted as: Teaching of the Word, baptism, Lord's Supper, prayer, worship, church discipline, giving, spiritual gifts, fellowship, evangelism, personal ministry to others. See Grudem, *Systematic*, 950-965 for a fuller description.

Chapter 7

United We Stand!

Any community or organisation, whether secular or religious, operates at its optimum efficiency when every member or adherent is unified in their common cause. Jesus confirms this in Luke 11:14-20, where the Gospel is under attack and the power of God is being questioned – this is an issue the church has had to face since the beginning. The public and private attacks on the authority of the word of God, the church and the person of God in general are becoming more apparent in an increasingly secular society. The words of Jesus in Luke 11:17 are as true of the divided church as it was when spoken; the church must be united as it embarks on the task of local, national and international mission. If the church congregants cannot be united in purpose due to the salvation received how can they ever be a powerful force in the world for the gospel?

The NT emphasises the necessity of striving for unity and presenting a united front for the gospel. Internal squabbles, deception, lies, back-biting and gossiping will only destroy individuals and ultimately the testimony of the church. There must be a concerted effort on behalf of the disciples of Jesus to know the biblical positions and stance of the local church on major issues of theology especially those which are under constant attack from a secular and humanistic society.

There is no place in the church for a 'loose canon' or someone who promotes their own ideas and portrays them as biblical. Although we must be careful not to produce corporate robots in our churches people should all have the same basic understanding of the word of God and it is interpretation in the 21st century otherwise as with the days of the Judges of the OT 'everyone does what is right in their own eyes'. Unity of purpose results from systematic teaching which sets the foundations and the boundaries for the actions of both individuals and congregation alike

The gospel records reveal a close-knit community of disciples and associates who stayed close together, united under the leadership of Jesus, (Luke 5:1-11, 27-28; Luke 6:12-16). These people drew close to the Lord Jesus and this interaction affected their ministry. It must be noted that the disciples were not perfect, and it is recorded that there were occasions when they disagreed or disputed an issue. Luke 9:46-47 and Luke 22:24-27 introduces the age-old issue of power and superiority and this following the most hallowed experiences of the transfiguration and the institution of the Lord's Supper. Why is it that we too can become so focussed on the carnal even following such spiritual highs? Here, Jesus had shared about the importance of his death, the new covenant and the cross; yet a group of men were more interested in their position, power and authority.

How often have you, following a time of fellowship where the blessing of God has been present turned on someone with an angry word, criticism or sarcastic remark? Beware, this is the seed of hatred and division which will bring people to a point of doubt, distrust and eventually could mar their spiritual development and enjoyment of God. Paul in Ephesians 4:1-3 emphasises the responsibility placed on everyone to play their part in maintaining unity in the body of Christ. Work on unity. Notice how he introduces this theme in verse 1-2, walking or living in a manner worthy of Jesus or in a Christ-like manner always showing preference to others; respecting them as people created in the image of God and saved by his grace alone.

Sometimes this act of maintaining unity requires people to work on their relationships, forgiveness, grace and to control their tongues. However, the rewards for the effort are always greater blessings from God. Return to Jesus and his dealings with those disciples in Luke 9:46-47 humility is the hallmark of true greatness in the kingdom of God. You may disagree with someone but talk about differences of opinion in a manner acceptable to the love of Christ in your heart. Luke presents a group of flawed disciples following Jesus endeavouring to learn from him and work for him in the world. Flawed disciples constitute the 21st century church; endeavour to learn and serve in a united manner.

The Book of Acts continues the picture of this group of disciples following on from the ascension of the Lord in a united fashion, supporting each other through the early years of the establishment of the church. This is a vital principle in the continuing story of the Christian faith.

Compare the following verses:

Acts 1:2-4, the apostles were together with the risen Lord, learning about the Kingdom. Here there is a principle provided for gathering together to learn, how the local church needs to return to being a earning community. For it is only a solid knowledge of the word of God and the principles of the Kingdom of God that will serve for the advancement of the church in the 21st century. The church in motion must be a church which is united on the solid, foundational and fundamental biblical tenets of the faith.

Acts 1:9-11, the disciples were together to witness the ascension of their Lord. Here is a key to evangelism: Jesus is not a dead historical figure but is living in the eternal realm. This is where Christianity differs from all other faiths and philosophies for it presents a living saviour. Again, the church must believe this principle and promote a living faith in a living Jesus.

Acts 1:15, they were united in their choice of Mattias. Often overlooked the issue of leadership selection is a key principle in unity. Here the apostles allowed God's will to be done in the selection of a replacement for Judas. People must be united on church policy; how things are done and who decisions are made are important. It is not good practice for people to use a system for church governance but then criticise it and complain that it is not correct because they did not get their own way.

Acts 1:14 and 2:1, gives two important phrases that express unity, *'all with one mind'*, and *'all together in one place'*. Here we see that both mental/spiritual and physical unity are necessary for the stability and growth of the local church.

The matter of unity is introduced through Luke's treatment of women and how he highlights their prominent role in the fledgling community. This revolutionary movement was to allow women the right to pray alongside men hence being involved in the direct ministry of the gospel (Acts 1:14). The cultural ethos of the day was being severely challenged by the new disciples and especially in the Lukan accounts of events in those formative years. Craig Blomberg states: 'Clearly Luke wants to highlight God's care for both genders and Jesus' concern to relate to both.'.[46]

This is further emphasised by Luke using the Joel quotation in Acts 2:17, where women are included amongst those affected by the Spirit and empowered to prophesy. Later in the narrative the reader is confronted with the daughters of

---

[46] Craig Blomberg, 'Women' in Elwell (Ed), *Evangelical Dictionary*, 824-828.

Philip who prophesied (Acts 21:8-9). Again, the emphasis is moving away from a male dominated religious hierarchy to include spiritual women used in spiritual ministry. This operation in the supernatural realm is not condemned either by the apostles or Luke, but there is an open acceptance of their role in ministry. The positive reference to Priscilla as a teacher of the word by Paul in Acts 18:24-28 underscores the view that women were not simply tolerated in the early church but encouraged to use the gifts distributed by the Spirit. This issue which has been much neglected in Evangelical circles until recent years requires further serious attention. It is clear to me that women were and should be an integral part of the operation of the local Christian community; and that not simply on a practical level. Remember that in the ancient world women held no position in society, the gospel came to set all free! (Acts 16:14-15).

Acts 6 introduces the 'social gospel' in relation to the widows who needed care, this matter was taken to heart by the church. The united community was not willing to see any suffer from lack of practical support, indeed, this disadvantaged group were sustained at the church's own expense. Once again, the revolutionary nature of the early gospel is highlighted whereby a much-maligned group – the widows – were elevated to a position of acceptance and concern for their well-being. The picture is being presented of a group of individuals who not only had a spiritual dynamism but also took their material and practical responsibilities very seriously.

The cameo of community life recorded in Acts 2:42-47 again highlights this practical issue as being a normal undertaking for the early church. The practical aspect of the gospel is one which can easily be overlooked in the local church; members can become so embroiled in petty pseudo-political, personality and other internal issues that the needs of their fellow worshippers can be forgotten. The social responsibility is described in Acts 2:41-46, Ernst Haenchen sums it up by stating:

> Whenever there is a need of money for the poor of the congregation, one of the property owners sells his piece of land or valuables, and the proceeds are given to the needy..[47]

This 'positive example of the earliest community of Christians'.[48] as Peterson puts it, is truly commendable and I concur with Peterson that this should be an

---

[47] Ernst Haenchen, *The Acts of the Apostles*, (Oxford: Blackwell, 1971), 192.
[48] Peterson, *Acts*, 158.

'example'. Therefore, the current Christian community should take note of this practical impact of those involved and consider whether there is any way in which this should affect their current thinking and practice. True fellowship is expressed in the recognition of someone's need and in the ability and priority to fulfil that need on the behalf of another. We must not though, read into this that everyone sold everything and lived in some form of primitive 'communism' this would have been impractical. However, as needs arose people with the ability to do so met the need through generosity of spirit that brought relief to the sufferer and glory to God..[49]

Perhaps, the political overtones should be removed from this aspect of sharing, however, it is true that such communal sharing was prominent in the embryonic church and a helpful aid in the spreading of the gospel. I submit that the major lesson for today's Christian communities is to re-examine one's financial commitment to the on-going cause of the gospel both on a local and international level. A major concern for me is that many of the younger generation (under 50's) appear to be less committed to financial sacrifice in order to support the work of God. There are, no doubt, many and varied personal reasons for people withholding finance however, none of them are totally legitimate as believers have a responsibility to financially support the ministry of the church. What is the answer to this lack of sacrificial giving? It must be that leaders teach about giving as an integral aspect of Christian worship also it is imperative that a compassionate ethos pervades the congregation.

The compassion of Christ led him to meet people's needs throughout his ministry the example of this is recorded in Luke 9:12-17. Here the actions of Jesus were not purely to demonstrate his power but also to illustrate his compassion. There is also the parable of the Good Samaritan in Luke 10:30-37.

The final challenge of Jesus to his disciples is; 'Go and do the same'. If there is any direct command to each generation of disciples to engage in social ministry, it must be this parable. This is further illustrated in Acts 4:32-36 where property was sold in order to help meet needs in the community and is continued as a

---

[49] I. Howard Marshall, *Acts,* (Leicester: IVP, 1996), 84-85 where Marshall suggests that this should not be understood as 'communism' due to the modern political connotations associated with the now failing political system which has become the total antithesis of Christianity.

biblical theme in 1 John 3:17-18 and 1 Corinthians 16:1-4. A vital matter to raise here is that those who received the funds – the Apostles – were spiritual people who had God's will at the heart of all their decision making on the use of funds. Local churches require similar spiritually minded people who deal with the funds and are open to the Lord's will to use his funds wisely for the purpose of ministry.

A brief mention of the importance of giving in the local assembly is required here, as it is a vital subject which is being neglected in the 21st century. At the outset it must be noted that a s a leader in the church and a former pastor I do not teach on giving as a means of seeking an increase in my wages; no pastor is ever paid enough for the responsibility placed on them for the role they fulfil (if fulfilled correctly). It is a common fallacy that all pastors should be kept poor in order to keep them humble, remember they too have bills to pay and children to put through university and also require times of relaxation a round of golf or a holidays for pastors are not a sin!

Giving, tithing, collections, offerings, call it what you will, the necessity is that all disciples of Jesus should give financially to the local church which they attend on a regular basis. There are many and varied unbiblical views on giving. The major ones being 'I'll give if I have anything left over' or 'I'll give a few coins I have loose in my pocket' or '£5 is ample to cover what it costs the church to have me there for an hour a week'. How sad that people take such a miserly attitude to giving to the Lord. Tithing the OT principle of giving a tenth of the income to the Lord's work is as far as I am concerned a minimum commitment for the NT Christian.

The OT was inadequate and demanded such giving by law, however, under the new covenant of grace we should be willing to give all to Jesus – an example as seen in the incident of the widow's mite (Luke 21:1-9). Here Jesus relates the story of a poor widow who gave a small offering however, it was not the size of the gift that mattered but the fact that it was *all she had to live on*. This is contrasted to the richer people who gave something, probably much more, but did this from a surplus of earnings.

The attitude of the giver is key here – are you willing to give all you have? Jesus is the ultimate example of giving: he gave his all for us why is it that we have decided to hold back finance from his work? Malachi sets the tone for the reason behind financial giving in Malachi 2:8-10 and reminds the reader that blessings occur when individuals give. The open windows of heaven represent the abundance of God in giving to his people (Psalm 78:23-24) however, it must be recognised what it is that God blesses his people with: spiritual blessings (Ephesians 1:3). Sadly modern Christianity has become infected with the disease of prosperity gospel teaching which relates giving to God to receiving more finance or health benefits. The Bible does not teach this, but the emphasis is upon receiving spiritual blessings form God for one's obedience to his commands. If the church can reclaim the vision of the importance of spiritual blessings and leave the materialistic attitude it has adopted in recent years, then it will begin to give to the Lord and receive the true blessings available from heaven.

Another major issue that requires attention and will release the blessings of God is, a move away from most Christians being 'takers' and not 'givers.' Let me explain. Too many people come to church to take or receive a spiritual injection to see them through another week, perhaps to enjoy the entertainment of a programme 'put on' by pastor and song leader. Sadly, the church is full of such people with an imbalanced view of church. Yes, we all hope and should expect to receive some spiritual help when we meet together, however, everyone should be willing to give or input into the local church situation through the giving of finance, time, effort, energy, spiritual diligence and spiritual support. All have gifts and all should be utilised in the progress of the gospel.

Giving whether finance or self should not be an afterthought but a priority. Do not give God your 'leftovers' but make financial commitment a priority, give to God first then see what is left for your entertainment, and if it means one meal less in your favourite restaurant just remember you are helping to see the gospel proclaimed and people's lives changed for eternity.

Paul highlights giving in 2 Corinthians 9 and he refers to it as a ministry.

1. How one 'sows' or gives can be either generously or miserly: the choice is yours (v6).
2. Give with joy and not grudgingly; remember the reason behind giving is to glorify God in Christ and through the proclamation of the gospel (v7). Again, the choice is yours.
3. Sufficiency for self is enough many Christians have far too much and waste so much (v8). Your giving could mean an abundance for someone else who currently has nothing. The choice is yours!
4. God is our ultimate example: God gives out of his abundance, will you? (v9). The choice is yours!

5. God supplies all your needs and allows for each person to have enough to live on (v10). The sad situation in our world is that humanity has abused nature and for political ends and due to corruption allows some to go hungry. I have always believed there is enough in the world if only people would drop their political agendas and focus on supporting others. Again, the choice is yours!

6. The result of giving is an inner enrichment or blessing from God, again something of which the modern Christian has lost sight (v11). Not only is the individual enriched spiritually they are also a channel to glorify God through thanksgiving.

7. Paul reminds the readers that giving is a ministry (v12). Romans 12:8 & 13 also refers to this spiritual ministry. Often gifts and ministries are viewed as the public or spectacular however, here giving is given an equal footing with teaching, prophecy etc.

8. Giving is a means of glorifying God in the lives of those who receive the material blessings of your generosity (v13).

9. Our puny human efforts to the ultimate example of Christ the *'indescrib*able' or *'unspeakable'* gift of God (v15). Or he of whom we could never find the words to tell of his generosity in giving himself for the world.

The embryonic Christian community as revealed in the NT was a generous body, people gave and things happened, blessings came, and the church grew both spiritually and numerically. Is that a paradigm that should be considered in the 21st century? I suggest it is vital to address the often-neglected ministry of giving. Can I urge you to consider regular committed giving, either weekly or monthly to your local church, decide today to give a set amount every month to the Lord's work – see this as your tithe. Then be a generous Christian and give on top of that to support missionaries, gospel outreach projects or social ministries as your offerings to the Lord's work as a thank you for what the Lord has done for you.

It is essential that any Christian community, that says it is Bible based, has a united heart for the cause of the gospel of the Lord Jesus Christ. This unity should be demonstrated in a united heart and vision and the financial commitment to see the work of God progress. It is unfortunate that as time has progressed that so-called Christians appear to have let this vital area of their lives slip, therefore becoming more concerned with self than with others. Psalm 133 provides a perfect reason for unity, blessing results! Ephesians 1:3 sets the divine standard, *'spiritual blessings'* and there are many recorded in Ephesians 1 such as grace, peace, our choice by God, adoption, forgiveness and redemption to name just a few. If we take Ephesians 1 as the standard for the type of blessings we desire and can receive it will radically adjust our expectations of blessing. Temporal issues must never be the driving force for acting out of one's Christianity; it must always be the promotion of the gospel and the glorifying of God. Seek the blessing of God and be a blessing to others.

It must also be noted that as the New Testament unfolds, we see the majority of epistles addressed to churches, not individuals, and the writers refer their readers to the necessity of unity in the church (Ephesians 4:1-3; Philippians 4:1; Colossians 3:12-14). One reality in the life of the church is that trouble will come across its path often this trouble is the cause of disunity in the congregation. In John 16:33 the Lord Jesus informs the disciples of the fact of future trouble. The church cannot afford to allow personality issues to cause dissent. Compare Acts 15:36-41; 1 Corinthians 1:11 and 3 John: 9-10. Are there any people in your church that you have a problem with that needs to be sorted out, do you have the grace to focus on unity and not disunity?

Consider the following problem: A person is angry because they have been overlooked for a position of leadership and is spreading gossip about the pastor and other leaders. How do you deal with this?

It often falls to the leaders to deal with matters of disunity but there is a biblical paradigm for coping with such issues. I label it as 'Quality Control.'

Quality Control!

How should a disciplinary matter be dealt with in the local church community?

There will be times when you will have to deal with serious matters, e.g. immorality or financial impropriety, it is essential that you deal with them in the biblical way! The Bible lays down principles for dealing with problematic church members.

Community discipline is essential, and all churches should have a disciplinary procedure in place and as part of its constitution. If this is the case, all members should be aware of this policy and therefore will not be able to complain when a decision is made.

What is a Framework for Discipline?

1. Brother to brother (Matthew 5:22-24; 1 Corinthians 5-6).
2. Two/three witnesses to the erring member (Matthew 18:15-16).
3. Pastor/elders to the erring member (Matthew 18:17; 1 Corinthians 1:11).
4. Excommunication for the unrepentant member (Matthew 18:17; 1 Timothy 1:20; 3 John: 9).
5. What about being accepted back, after genuine repentance?

See also, Ezra 10:1-18; John 9:22-34; 2 Thessalonians 3:6-15; Titus 3:10-11; 1 Timothy 5:20; 1 Corinthians 11:30; Revelation 2:20-22.

Note!

Serious matters of discipline will be few and far between, be sure that no one 'lords' it over a congregation, and hence have a rule for the most insignificant matters and take joy out of discipline. Regular biblical preaching and teaching should be enough to encourage people to live as Christians, the emphasis should be placed on good solid biblical instruction, then allow the convicting power of the Holy Spirit to work on people's hearts and minds to change them in God's time. Enforced restrictions can sometimes prove negative!

The whole matter of discipline needs to be treated with the respect it deserves, remember not to discuss the 'issues' openly when other people's lives are involved, we are not to be gossips. Discernment is essential in all such matters, (Matthew 7:3); judging others can be a big problem.[50] I have also learned from experience the necessity to make a brief public statement when a serious issue of discipline is required. This allows for the membership to be fully informed as to the reason the church leaders have decided and taken the stance. This will prevent unnecessary gossip, assumptions and hopefully discourage further serious issues to be raised in the church.

Leaders be prepared to act but do not go looking for trouble!

---

[50] See 1 Corinthians 4:5; 1 Corinthians 6:1; 1 Peter 4:15; Ephesians 4:32; Galatians 6:1.

Think it Over!

Do you belong to a church body that is united in purpose?

Are you holding a grudge against anyone which is holding back the blessing of God?

Do you desire spiritual blessings or material gain?

Are you a generous Christian who gives to the glory of God?

Chapter 8

All Together in Fellowship

So when they had come together, they asked him, 'Lord will you at this time restore the kingdom to Israel?' Acts 1:6

The early Christian community was one that met together regularly, probably daily, for spiritual fellowship. Fellowship means, companionship, a relation of parties which hold something in common, 'to share with someone in something' or 'to give someone a share in something'..[51] True fellowship therefore can only occur when those involved hold the same values; this is illustrated in 1 John 1:3. Here the writer emphasises that the fellowship between people emerges from the fellowship that the individuals have with *'the Father'*. Fellowship, therefore, emanates from the fact that the believer is joined in spiritual union with Christ to the Father and to each other true believer. Further development of this theme is seen in John 15:1-11 where the aspect of abiding in Christ (having true fellowship with him) is the duty of the branch (disciple). The result of this abiding or spiritual fellowship is the production of spiritual fruit which is only possible as the disciple draws strength and life from the true vine – Christ.

Paul highlights the necessity of spiritual fruit in Galatians 5:22-25 and this is a direct result of the indwelling Holy Spirit and suggests a life of spiritual fruitfulness can only be achieved as the 'old life' of sin is defeated and a greater union with God through the Spirit is achieved. Therefore, every individual in Christ is also in fellowship with the Father and each other as a result one's actions can directly affect other disciples; hence the necessity of watchfulness in life so as to prevent others from missing out in the realm of spiritual growth through flippant attitudes to the pursuit of holiness.

Fellowship is essential for spiritual survival, growth and impacting the wider community. There is a common misconception that fellowship means meeting for a coffee and chat; that is an aspect of fellowship, as too is gathering with

---

[51] Peterson, *The Acts of the Apostles*, 160.

friends for a meal. However, this must never replace the true spiritual fellowship that is gained from meeting together to engage in corporate worship, prayer, singing, listening to the preaching and waiting on God: this is the source of all other aspects of fellowship. Do not be like the Hebrew readers who were forsaking assembling together (Hebrews 10:23-25). The church must be united and fellowshipping together to be more effective in the work of the gospel. Yes, enjoy the company of fellow believers, but do not allow that to replace meeting together with the Lord the source of our common spiritual life and purpose.

Luke-Acts stresses the fundamental importance of fellowship in the Christian community. Luke proceeds from his gospel and the picture of Jesus with a very small community of followers to Acts and a group of people who are now minus their leader. This remaining group are totally dependent upon each other for help, support, knowledge, accountability and direction; true biblical fellowship is therefore a necessity. The great news for all disciples is that Jesus has not left them alone but through the Holy Spirit is ever present, another emphasis of Luke as mentioned in Part 2.

Fellowship in the Gospel of Luke

The purpose of the gospel is to affect the growth of a new Christian community. Jesus said he would 'build his church' this picture represents the necessity of bringing people together as one. 1 Peter 2:4-5 reiterate this fact and emphasises the spiritual nature of the people who constitute the church, not the building, time or programmes, but the people. If the 'structure' is to be solid, it must firstly be built on good foundation, the word of God and be constituted of spiritually alive people working close together and bringing mutual support (Ephesians 2:19-22). The church must be united in fellowship as a result of the gospel message this unity expressed in Luke 2:32 initially brings people from different social backgrounds (Jews and Gentiles) together in faith. This then is the foundation for the biblical fellowship necessary between people brought from different backgrounds to serve the Lord.

The first significant illustration of fellowship is recorded in Luke 5:1-11 where the first disciples are called to follow Jesus in his earthly ministry. Matthew (Levi) is called in Luke 5:27 to 'follow' Jesus and join the fellowship group growing around the new rabbi. Luke 6:12-19 brings the choosing of the Twelve to the forefront. This group sets the standard for the on-going fellowship of disciples throughout history. These disciples were chosen in order to be with Jesus and to learn of his teaching and ways; this represents how fellowship today should work; firstly one must be close to Christ, then secondly learning the teachings of the Gospel in order to affect society, and finally close to each other for mutual support.

There is an interesting phrase often neglected found in Luke 8:3 *'who were contributing to their support out of their private means.'* This reference to a group of women who followed Jesus and the disciples is a precursor of what becomes more widely apparent in Acts. These women supported the missionary activity of the new group of the traveling teacher joining in fellowship with them and assisting in whatever way possible (here through financial support). As will be dealt with below this practical aspect of the gospel became more prominent in Acts.

The Christian community requires financial support in order to survive, pastors, teachers, itinerant workers, and missionaries all require finance to live and work. If these people are going to fulfil their calling you may need to financially support their work. Jesus continues to teach about the practical aspect of true fellowship i.e. recognising needs and meeting them in Luke 12:33. Here, the encouragement to the Disciples of Christ is to be involved in charitable work' this social concern was a particular interest to Luke however, the fact that Jesus taught it must require closer attention from 21st century Christians.

Two Main Divisions of Fellowship in Acts

1. Physical fellowship simply being together (Acts 2:1).
2. Spiritual fellowship being united in the things of God (Acts 1:14).

Acts 2:42, states that fellowship was an integral part of church life and is listed alongside, the word of God, prayer and breaking of bread; it must be considered as one of the pillars of the local assembly.

The believers met together in order to:

1. Learn (Acts 1:3).
2. Pray (Acts 1:14).
3. Share (Acts 4:32-36 the practical gospel).
4. To eat the Lord's supper (Acts 2:42; 1 Corinthians 11:17-33).
5. To praise/worship (Ephesians 5:19).

Luke is at pains to demonstrate that the new community is seen to be together in all things. They meet together as a group to learn more about their new faith, to make decisions and to meet practical needs.

Think it Over!

How do you define fellowship?

Is being together enough?

Should all Christian fellowship contain some biblical element?

What importance to you place by the spiritual act of fellowship?

How can one promote true fellowship in the modern church?

Do you engage in social ministry as part of your local mission?

Chapter 9

Everyone in the Pool: Water Baptism

And they both went down into the water, Philip and the eunuch, and he baptised him.
Acts 8:38

There is much debate over the process of water baptism throughout the Christian church, these range from infant baptism to adult believer baptism. From the outset I must nail my colours to the mast and state I believe in full immersion of all true believers. I realise this may not be everyone's interpretation however, a look at the NT should convince people of this interpretation and practice. I have many memories of baptismal services at my home church as a child, a testimony from the candidate, usually dressed in a white robe who then proceeded to the pool where the pastor and an elder would baptise on the confession of their faith. Following their immersion, a favourite chorus would be sung by the congregation as they extricated themselves from the pool dripping in water but radiant in the fact they had 'followed Jesus through the water'. This practice was, and still is, the way many evangelical churches conduct baptism. The key element being the individual's ability to state they had a real conversion experience and this act was a personal choice and not a ritual imposed by parents. The debate continues!

The subject of water baptism is introduced in Luke 3:21-22 and Acts 1:5. Notice the work of John was not condemned but accepted as a proper part of Christian salvation (Acts 1:22). The matter of water baptism is not superseded by the arrival of the Lord Jesus, but He actually gives His approval by undergoing the rite at the hands of John (Luke 3). This pattern then, is one that we should follow. It is an area of our Christian experience that we see carried on throughout the New Testament (1 Corinthians 1:10-17). Paul and other NT apostles and leaders were keen to see new believers make a public show of their faith by undergoing the rite of baptism.

Acts 2:38, Peter tells his hearers of the need for baptism following salvation.
Acts 8:34-40, Philip baptised the Ethiopian on the confession of his faith.
Acts 10:44-48, the household of Cornelius was baptised.

The incident in Acts 8, is very important in the teaching of baptism. Philip obviously mentioned the matter of baptism in his 'evangelistic sermon', because as soon as they found water, the Ethiopian asked for baptism. Notice the one condition for allowing someone to be baptised is belief in the Lord Jesus, as the Son of God! (Acts 8:37).

Baptism is derived from the Greek word 'baptizo', meaning to 'dip/immerse', and therefore should always be carried out in water, that is by complete immersion.[52]

The New Testament sets out water baptism as a necessity in the life of a believer:

1. Matthew 3:13-17.
2. Romans 6:3-5.
3. Colossians 2:11-12.

Salvation is not attained by baptism; it is purely the outward show of faith in the Lord Jesus Christ as saviour. This is where those who believe only believer baptism place their belief, as the thinking is that no one can decide if another person, especially a baby/infant, should be baptised, as this removes the whole issue of individual faith and decision to follow Jesus. I have though known of churches which operate both models, i.e. they believed in infant baptism as a form of christening, but also provided for people to be fully immersed at a later date upon their personal confession of faith. This, to me, is a little bizarre or one may suggest they are 'covering all their bases' and hence not offending anyone. Of course, the major problem with this practice is determining who is truly baptised. A dilemma that I still have!

Think it Over

Look at the verses above and examine the type and role of baptism in the life of the early church?

Do you recognise the need of water baptism?

Have you been baptised?

---

[52] Stephen Gaukroger, *Being Baptised: The Believers Handbook to Baptism* (Pontypool: Faithbuilders, 2019); Tim Chester, *Preparing for Baptism* (The Good Book Company, 2017).

Chapter 10

A Meal for All Time: Breaking of Bread

And he took bread, and when he had given thanks, he broke it and gave it to them
Luke 22:19

Food plays an important role in the biblical narrative. The problems in Genesis 3 resulted from Adam and Eve desiring some fruit; Genesis 18 relates how Abraham made a meal for the angelic visitors; Moses is instructed to hold the Passover meal in Exodus 12; Ruth and Boaz are united over the former's need of food.

In the NT food continues to be central to the narrative. Luke 7 sees Jesus a guest of a Pharisee at a meal; five thousand are fed in Luke 9; Jesus reveals himself to the two disciples at Emmaus over a meal in Luke 24.

Food is important in the biblical narrative and still plays a vital role in many cultures sadly in our western culture, fast food, microwave dinners and instant noodles have detracted from the quality time we should spend as families and with friends around the dining table. Perhaps the change in our social culture is a story for another place, however, could our western instant society be affecting the churches understanding of the solemnity of the Lord's Table/Communion as instituted in the NT by Jesus?

The Breaking of Bread was instituted by Jesus during the Last Supper, passed onto the Early Church and hence to each succeeding generation of Christians (Luke 22:14-23; Acts 2:42). Other titles used are, Eucharist (giving of thanks), Lord's Supper, Table of the Lord or Communion (fellowship or festival in common).[53] It is known as one of the 'sacraments' – or 'oath of enlistment' – along with Water Baptism.

---

[53] David Allen, *Neglected Feast*, (Nottingham: New Life, 2007); Robert Letham, *The Lord's Supper Eternal Word in Broken Bread*, (Phillipsburg: PandR Publishing, 2001).

89

Jesus set in order the Breaking of Bread before His death and this took place at the same time as the Jewish Passover (cf. Exodus 12-13). Parts of the communion service are seen to symbolically replace some aspects of the Passover, especially the fact that Jesus is seen as the sacrificial lamb, given for the sin of mankind. The origins are recorded in Matthew 26:26-29; Mark 14:22-25; Luke 22:19-20. Paul also records a divine revelation of the true aspects of communion in 1 Corinthians 11:23-34.

It is interesting that John does not record the details of the Last Supper in his gospel; however, in chapter 13 he does relate important attitudes of heart which should accompany any celebration of this rite. For John the mechanics are not so important, but the heart is, servanthood, love and commitment are necessary as he reflects on the seriousness of the Lord's Supper. I submit we should not get obsessed with the traditional mechanics and focus on matters of the heart which are far more important and relevant to the ceremony. However, I do believe there should be an element of awe, respect, quietness and contemplation during the communion service. This is because of the focus of the act being the very real and highly important issue of Christ's death and our forgiveness, if we trivialise those vital aspects, we are doing a major disservice to the Lord Jesus who suffered so much for our salvation.

Awe, respect and humility should characterise the communion service and I also submit that churches should devote more time to this sacred act as it is one of the commands that Jesus left us, we emphasise singing and would never think of not having at least four songs in every service however, we can be prone to slot communion into a five minute period at the end of the 'worship' purely as a habitual ritual and miss the solemnity of the practice and the focus upon Jesus. Remember: Luke-Acts is 'all about Jesus' and so should the Christian life and the corporate worship of the local church.

The symbolic meaning of the communion is to remind us of the sacrificial work of Christ and what he achieved by his sufferings. There is no mystical power in the bread or wine; these are simply emblems to help focus our minds on the true work of Christ. What Jesus was doing that night in the Upper Room was implementing the New Covenant between man and God through his blood. It was now by faith in him and his death and resurrection that people could enjoy true fellowship with God. The Old Covenant, i.e. the OT sacrificial system was now surpassed by Jesus he was the one perfect sacrifice for the sin of humanity. This was a once for all act there was no longer any need of daily or annual sacrifice in order to appease God.

1 Corinthians 11:23-34 provides more insight into the actual details of the Communion service. There are some very important aspect for the believer's responsibility in respect to the Table of the Lord.

1. It is a new covenant (v25).

2. It is a time of remembrance (v24-25).

3. It is a time of preparation (v28).

4. It is a time of proclamation/witness (v26).

5. It is a time of expectation (v26).

Communion should not just be a solemn time as there is much hope for the communicant. This is where the celebration of forgiven sin and expected joy in the anticipated return of Jesus occurs. However, it is not a time to disregard the seriousness of the crucifixion and the humility and humiliation of Jesus in this act. More time should be devoted to the Breaking of Bread with a greater realisation of what it represents and remembers. It is essential that this rite is observed with the correct spiritual attitude and does not become too familiar with its occurrence; this is not a time filler in the morning service! Regular observance keeps the reality of Jesus fresh in our minds.

Think it Over!

Do you attend Communion on a regular basis?

How important is it that we remember the atoning work of Christ on a regular basis?

Do you prepare yourself –spiritually- before you receive the bread and wine?

Chapter 11

Any Volunteers! Church Organisation

Therefore, brothers, pick out from among you seven men of good repute, full of the Spirit and of wisdom, whom we will appoint to this duty. Acts 6:3

The 'Cinderella syndrome' or the things that are often overlooked as unimportant, yet they are vital to the progress of any organisation is often a problem in local churches. Luke-Acts introduces a major 'Cinderella' issue: Church Organisation, if the church is to grow and function in a biblical manner it must be organised along biblical lines. Sadly, too many churches are being badly managed and organised there being little structure and even less accountability. I make a call for more 'joined up church' where all the people, departments and ministries are functioning in a complimentary manner for the extension of the kingdom, whether the church is together in corporate worship or scattered among the community at school, work or leisure.[54]

The major issue of ecclesiology, the study of the church or 'called out ones', is vital as we endeavour to uncover the central themes in Luke's writing. John Stott writes:

> We urgently need a healthy, biblical understanding of the church, for only then shall we have a healthy, biblical understanding of Christian leadership.[55]

Stott provokes a serious issue in a major rethink of leadership and organisation which entails addressing the major issue of what is the church and its purpose. These major questions will impact every local church as it endeavours to reshape its focus in the 21st century. Is it time for the church to be revolutionised and its leadership to be refocussed on biblical principles and not be left simply to the volunteers? Some of the more technical, perhaps often overlooked, yet

---

[54] Hudson, *Imagine Church*, for a more detailed appreciation of this vital subject and attitude.

[55] John Stott, *Basic Christian Leadership*, (Downers Grove, IL: IVP, 2002) 93.

vital elements of early church life are described by Luke.[56] Jesus chose twelve disciples in order that they may be with him, learn the principles of the Kingdom of God and then take the gospel message to the wider world. This theme of correct leadership is seen throughout the biblical narrative and is essential to the successful presentation of the gospel in the local Christian community.[57]

Old and New

The relation between the Old Israel and the new Church is of interest in Luke; it is probably correct to trace a link between old Israel and the new faith from the birth narratives. In Luke 1-3, Zechariah, Elizabeth and John represent God's dealings with the people Israel. Luke sets the scene:

Zechariah is in the Temple (Luke 1:8 the central focus of OT ritual worship).

Jesus is brought to the Temple to fulfil the requirements of the law of circumcision (Luke 2:21-24 & 39). Luke refers to the OT scriptures as the context for the narrative and all the events surrounding the birth narratives are recorded in OT prophesy (Luke 2:32; Luke 3:4-6).

It is essential for the Bible student to recognise the essential role played by the OT in the NT narrative. The foundations on which the revelation of the gospel is made is the OT prophetic word. God was at work from the beginning Genesis 3 to provide humanity with an escape route from the effects of sin; this would be fulfilled in Jesus. Do not neglect the OT in your personal devotions; there is much depth of meaning found in its pages also make Hebrews a book of serious study as the writer puts much of the OT ritual into the context of Jesus. The old and new are inescapably linked and even though the New Covenant now dominates the Christian theological scene, the Old Covenant must never be forgotten.

However, the break with the OT is made when Jesus commences his ministry:

---

[56] John Balchin, *I Want To Know What The Bible Says About The Church,* (Eastbourne: Kingsway, 1979); G.C. Berkouwer, *The Church,* (Grand Rapids: Eerdmans, 1976); Karkkainen, Veli-Matti, *An Introduction to Ecclesiology,* (Downers Grove: IVP, 2002).
[57] Paul Beasley-Murray, *Dynamic Leadership,* (Eastbourne: Monarch (MARC) 1990); Chris Palmer, *Essential Christian Leadership,* (London: Faithbuilders, 2019); J. Oswald Sanders, *Spiritual Leadership,* (Chicago: Moody Press, 1994).

John introduces the Spirit (Luke 3:16) and a change of emphasis in the message of the new order of Christ.

Jesus states clearly his mission in the context of OT fulfilment (Luke 4:17-21). The ministry of Jesus was to focus on a message of release, freedom and care; the church eventually would be the conduit for the blessing of the gospel to flow into the whole world. This would be the culmination of the promise to Abraham in Genesis 12:1-3.

The early chapters of Luke's gospel set the scene for a change in the focus of the theological world; Jerusalem the city of God was no longer the focus; Jesus the son of God was now paramount, and the world was his parish.

Disciples

As the story unfolds so we encounter the church emerging or becoming a distinct separate entity from the old system of Israelite worship. This is seen in the appointment of the disciples in Luke 5:1-10 & 27-30 and Luke 6:12-16.

These were overall uneducated men, outcasts from normal accepted society, ceremonially unacceptable – not the typical leaders of Jewish religious orders. However, Jesus and his message came to change perspectives his first major issue was to show his impartiality and that even the lowest in rank could serve in his kingdom. Mere fishermen were considered worthy to carry the message of the gospel.[58] For most of the gospel Luke emphasises the work of Jesus however we get glimpses of the disciples being involved in various tasks:

> Luke 9:1-11 - they had a message to proclaim, the KOG, and heal people – the miraculous is of interest to Luke the doctor.
> Luke 10:1-29 - the enlarged ministry team of 70 (72) sent out on mission again. v17 miraculous incidents a great importance and note the response of Jesus. v20 notes we must never exalt the miraculous to a place higher than salvation!
> Luke 22:24-62 - the weakness of human flesh the chosen followers had deserted Jesus in his time of need only Peter followed for a brief time

---

[58] It has been my privilege to enjoy a good education culminating in the awarding of a PhD in 2014 however, I do not believe that gospel ministry is the preserve of the educated; all disciples whatever their level of learning and understanding are called to take the message to the nations.

then he too succumbed to the pressure, fear, doubt and disappointment. Be careful not to condemn Peter alone, we are told all the disciples forsook Jesus in his hour of greatest need.

Luke 24:13-49 - Jesus does not forget his followers however desperate they became he was there for their help, instruction, comfort and guidance.

The Church Age?

Acts introduces the reader to the Church age as Kee writes:

> The launching and supervision of the community reaching out into the wider Roman world is the work of the apostles, although they recede in importance as the story progresses.[59]

Kee may be exaggerating the loss in importance of the apostles as Acts 15 describes the centrality of their role in major decision making. However, he is correct in the fact that Luke emphasises the role of Paul following his conversion this is probably because he was acquainted with him on his missionary journeys. Kee further neglects the probable reason behind Luke's account in Acts as focussing on Paul and his ministry input for a specific reason, as noted above. Furthermore, as Bruce comments it is interesting that from Acts 9 on only Peter, James and John of the original list in Acts 1:13 are mentioned again. These central figures become increasingly important in the leadership and organisation of the embryonic Christian communities. Leadership generally falls into the hands of a few God raised up individuals, how such God ordained people are required in the 21st century.

The sceptic may simply say Luke was recording a biography of his hero Paul this may well be true but there could be many reasons for this as I mentioned in Part 1 of this book. Whatever, the reason in Acts the reader is confronted with a new body of believers setting out on a journey of faith and overcoming problems, issues, disagreements et al along the way. Luke has done the Christian church a great service by recording how the 'nuts and bolts' of the early church fixed together to form a cohesive mass moving outward for the sake of the gospel.

---

[59] Kee, *Good News*, 70.

Leadership and Organisation in the Early Church

The apostles, from the very beginning of their leadership responsibilities, saw the need to get the right people in the right positions. Often the choice of leaders is a crucial aspect in church life.

The following references refer to the importance of organisation:

> Acts 1:12ff - structured leadership in finding a replacement for Judas.
> Acts 2:14 - strong leadership, with Peter the spokesman for the group.
> Acts 6:1-7 - the choice of deacons: servanthood in leadership and the spiritual priority of the Apostles being to devote themselves to prayer and the word. The church requires leaders saturated in prayer and the word.
> Acts 11:1-18 and Acts 13 & 15 - a base for the church: we all need a home church. Leadership decisions must be made and cascaded to the congregation.

We must realise that there is no one person or group of people that hold all the gifts/abilities in the local church, but ultimately the pastor/elders have final responsibility. Notice how even Paul, returned to Antioch and Jerusalem in order to report home! Accountability in spiritual leadership is imperative.

The NT church operated a very well organised structure, elders and deacons appear to be the main positions of responsibility. However, in Acts, the Apostles were the leaders and their authority spread throughout the early ages of Christianity (Acts 15; 20:17-38 and compare 1 Timothy 3 and Titus 1:5-9)..[60]

Luke presents a picture of the church led by Apostles – men of authority assisted by 'deacons' or 'almoners' (Acts 6). However, there was no one person with all authority the burden did not fall on one person in matters of leadership, decision making and operations – the load was shared.

As we progress through the NT, we see positions such as apostles, prophets, evangelists, pastors and teachers as gifts of Christ to the Church and should be given the respect they deserve (Ephesians 4:11). One is also confronted with elders and deacons who should be held in high regard due to the work they

---

[60] Chris Palmer, *The Pastoral Epistles: A Course Study in Practical Theology* (London: Faithbuilders, 2016). Palmer, *Essential*.

carry out for the church (1 Timothy and Titus give further information on these roles).

Space does not allow for these positions of leadership to be considered in any detail. However, it is necessary that the church is made aware of the fact that the early church was well organised in both spiritual and practical matters. I have a major concern about the organisation and especially the leadership of local churches, and that is the apparent emphasis in churches of finding managers and not pastors. I have expressed this concern in my *Essential Christian Leadership*:

> In the Christian church, the role of the leader should never be confused with the role of manager. In the Bible, Christian leaders are instead compared to shepherds, who are chosen by God to lead, protect and help the people of God grow. What the 21st century church requires are shepherd-leaders who are focussed on God….[61]

The Church in Luke-Acts a Summary Acts 2:41-47

1. Led by spiritual people answerable to God.

2. Spirit filled.

3. Worshipping group.

4. Learning group.

5. Loving group.

6. Caring group.

7. Sharing group.

8. Powerful group.

9. Happy group.

---

[61] Palmer, *Essential*, 11, I accept that the church must be well managed however, the pastor who should know what is going on should be confident to leave the organising of events, programmes and other non-critical issues to the church secretary or other members of the leadership team/church council/board. Some pastors appear to be nothing more than 'control freaks' who follow their own agenda and impose their views by becoming dictatorial managers rather than caring shepherds.

Think it Over!

How can we assess the role of local leaders today in light of Luke-Acts?

Is there a definite structure of leadership?

Do you need to reassess your view of leadership considering Luke-Acts?

Thoughts

Often the disciple of Jesus is only interested in the feelings of a spiritual life or experiencing the joys of spiritual victories. However, it is a reality that the church must function on a day to day basis with often very practical issues to address therefore good organisation is required. Those called to lead are only called and equipped by God and if they are, they should be allowed to lead in the way God is directing them and the church should support them in all they do for the gospel.

This section has dealt with some of those very practical but obviously necessary issues facing every church congregation and they range from the very spiritual aspects of baptism and breaking of bread to the more mundane organisational issues. However, all are vital if the church is going to progress and grow in the things of God. It may be a good time to stop and consider where you are and where your church is going in relation to some of these fundamental issues. Why not call the church together and discuss where you are going in God's plans and purposes and perhaps determine to seek God more earnestly for his will? The world needs a church that is well led, spiritually focussed and moving forward in God. Are you a part of such a church?

Part 2B

The Christian Community in Action

Introduction

As they ministered to the Lord and fasted, the Holy Spirit said; 'Now separate to Me Barnabas and Saul for the work to which I have called them. Acts 13:2

The title of this book is 'Acting Out Your Christianity'. I chose this because I firmly believe Christianity is a religion that calls for its adherents to outwork their faith through a variety of avenues. The NT calls attention to the 'works' that the Christian disciple should be involved with daily. Ephesians 4:11-12 instructs leaders to prepare others for general works of ministry or service. James 2:14-26 emphasises the necessity of works flowing from the faith that saves. As you read this Part devote some time to thinking about what you are doing as a result of being a follower of Jesus. Christianity and the church are not spectator sports but something that requires active participation from every member for the gospel to flourish.

A common theme in the NT is that of the church as a body and 1 Corinthians 12-14 highlights this issue. The over-riding thought of this analogy is that all bodies only function at their optimum when every part is operating to its fullest potential and concentrating on the reason it exists. Therefore, when it comes to the local Christian community each member, or body part, must focus on its ministry and then the body will make progress. If there is a fault or a 'schism', as Paul says in 1 Corinthians 12:25, then this will cause a lack of progress can and will lead to disharmony and probable ineffective service.

Therefore, the leaders of the church must be people who teach and practice the necessity of unity and encourage everyone to discover their ministry and to release them to fulfil that ministry within the local church and wider community. A church in which every member of the body is not functioning is struggling to be a biblical based, vital and productive entity. The Bible is a book of action; God's action on behalf of his creation, and creations action on behalf of its God. Luke-Acts records a vibrant, vital and very active church the following are some insights into the importance of being a Christian Community in Action.

Before you proceed through the next few chapters consider your role in the local church. Are you fulfilling the calling God has placed on your life? This does not have to be a call to live in another country as a missionary to the unreached people groups. Neither does it mean you are to enter full time paid Christian ministry as a pastor, it simply means you are serving the Lord in some capacity or another that is essential to the forward progress of the body of Christ where he has placed you for his glory. You have the choice will you act out your Christianity or will you sit back and wait for others to fill the you shaped gap?

Chapter 12

It's Not Magic: It's a Miracle

But Peter said, 'I have no silver and gold, but what I do have I give to you. In the name of Jesus Christ of Nazareth, rise up and walk'. Acts 3:6

An important theme and interest for Luke-Acts is the miraculous; it is accepted that Luke was a medical person with an interest in healing, and this becomes very apparent in his treatment of the ministry of Jesus and the Apostles. The miraculous is not simply confined to acts of healing there are various power encounters that Luke emphasises in order to illustrate the power of the gospel. These can be highlighted from both the ministry of Jesus and the Apostles. The question to consider through this area of study is: what is the place of the miraculous today?[62]

Miraculous/Spectacular in the Gospel of Luke

The miraculous commences with the birth narratives as the reader encounters a miraculous God working within the human bodies of Elizabeth is barren and old (Luke 1:7) and Mary a virgin and unmarried (Luke 1:26-35). God's power is demonstrated in two supposed humanly impossible situations. One major issue when considering the miraculous is to understand that it is, the work of God outside of the usual parameters of human activity bringing about an unexpected or humanly impossible result. This is perhaps why some struggle with the whole issue of the miraculous, in that they cannot see anything happening outside the normal human existence or 'laws of nature'.

Zechariah also experiences the raw power of God (Luke 1:18-22, 67-79). This had a visible impact upon him but also brought awareness of the divine power to those who witnessed his speechlessness. This is further highlighted at the birth

---

[62] Wayne Grudem (Ed), *Are Miraculous Gifts For Today?* (Grand Rapids: Zondervan, 1996); Ronald Kydd, *Charismatic Gifts in the Early Church,* (Peabody: Hendrickson, 1984); David Petts, *Just a Taste of Heaven* (Mattersey: Mattersey Hall, 2006).

of Zechariah and Elizabeth's son when the father's tongue is loosed, and praise is given to God (Luke 1:57-66).

The supernatural appearance of the angelic hosts proclaiming the birth of Jesus again highlights this miraculous power at work (Luke 2:9-15). Angels are associated with divine visitations and are certainly outside of the normal human experience. Luke uses this event to highlight and build the story of the revelation of a miraculous God throughout his account.

Two individuals are prompted by miraculous/supernatural power to visit the Temple environs at the exact time the baby Jesus is brought to fulfil the legal requirements. Simeon and Anna come to the Temple through the miraculous power of the Spirit prompting them to speak out prophetically regarding the future ministry of the child (Luke 2:25-38). The prophecy of Simeon also introduces one of Luke's major themes, the inclusion of the Gentiles in the mission of God through the Gospel of Jesus (Luke 2:32).

The Temptation of Jesus recorded in Luke 4:1-13 reveals the power of God at work through his Son in conflict with the devil. This is an on-going issue throughout Luke-Acts; the confrontation between the truth of Christ and the lies of the devil. There is a real enemy at work in the world and this is something that Luke endeavours to highlight to prepare his readers for the spiritual battle which faces them daily. It is only through the miraculous power of God through his word that the disciple can survive the intense spiritual battles faced in their daily walk.

The ultimate example for all subsequent Christian ministry and service is the Lord Jesus himself, Luke-Acts introduces a Jesus with a miraculous public ministry (Luke 4:18-19). This summary of the ministry of Jesus introduces us to the battle in the spiritual places and includes Jesus healing a variety of afflictions and performing various powerful acts:

> Healings (Luke 4:38; Luke 5:12-26; Luke 7:1-17).
> Power over death (Luke 7:22; Luke 8:49-56).
> Control over nature (Luke 8:22-25; Luke 9:12-27).
> Control over the spirit world (Luke 4:41; Luke 8:26-39).
> Empowerment of followers to be involved in similar ministry (Luke 10:1-16).

However, a word of caution is necessary here as Luke 10:19-20 provide the correct perspective. Even though the miraculous is desirable and beneficial to the ongoing work of the gospel, this is not a cause to rejoice, for true joy and excitement comes from the miracle of salvation and not the acquisition or manifestation of the miraculous power. Can I suggest that perhaps recently too many have exalted the power and the miraculous over and against the purpose they serve in bringing glory to God and directing people to follow the gospel as a step on the pathway towards salvation.

These incidents all refer the reader to the power of God at work through Jesus and the embryonic Christian community. In the gospel narrative healings and demonstrations of power emphasise and highlights the true divinity and person of Jesus. He operates in the power of the Spirit as the one who has the authority to deal with natural ailments and supernatural afflictions. These supernatural power encounters are testimony to his role and purpose of initiating the Kingdom of God on earth and commencing a new era in the work of God on earth. John 20:30-31 provides an excellent summary of the purpose of the miraculous ministry of Jesus:

> Now Jesus did many other signs in the presence of the disciples, which are not written in this book; but these are written so that you may believe that Jesus is the Christ the son of God, and that by believing you may have life in his name.

Therefore, it is correct to state that, the reason for the miraculous ministry of Jesus was to prove his Messiahship, divinity and that through these demonstrations, faith may be formed in the observer. Again, it is imperative to note that the miraculous was not present simply for the spectacular effect but to draw people to the message of the truth of the gospel found in Christ.

However, what would happen once Jesus had ascended to heaven? Did the miraculous end and serve no further purpose in the life of the embryonic church? According to the Luke-Acts narrative this miraculous, supernatural empowerment is as available for the disciples as it was for Jesus.

The Miraculous in Acts

The miraculous in Acts takes on less significance than in the gospel, the centre of attention is no longer proving the reliability of the message and messenger, Jesus. However, it is to illustrate that he continues to work through his followers in power and authority. As Warrington states: 'To suggest that the healings were the norm would not be reflective of the message of Acts'.[63] This is a hypothesis based upon the fact that Luke records far fewer healings, exorcisms and miracles in Acts than he does in the gospel. This could be for the following reasons. Firstly, the miracles were simply less in number. Secondly, miraculous events were accepted as norm in the early church hence Luke saw no need to record all their occurrences. Thirdly, the miracles recorded were to illustrate certain issues that required re-emphasising in the early church. Fourthly, there is a different priority in Acts than in the gospel, which is the focus being on the spread of the gospel around the Mediterranean basin through the preaching of the word through the indwelling Holy Spirit.

However, it must be recognised that according to Acts 2:43, *'signs and wonders'*, or supernatural acts followed the preaching of the word. This is an important aspect of the preaching of the gospel, furthermore the words of the Jesus see their fulfilment in the working of the apostles (Mark 16:15-18). These miracles were there to serve as further proof of the definite divine source of the gospel message and were not the central issue. It must be remembered here that Luke, when writing, could not include every detail of the apostolic ministry, time and space would not allow. Luke though is able in a few short passages to show that the miraculous did occur and that it was expected by the apostles.

Acts 3:1-10 are important verses in our understanding of this divine operation through the apostles. The lame man was healed at the temple gate, notice:

> v6 - total dependence on God.
> v6 - calling on the name of God/Jesus.
> v9 - the Lord deserves the praise and glory.[64]

Here we are confronted with a picture of the centrality of Jesus in healing, the apostles are simply continuing the message and acts of Jesus. It is vital that the reader of Acts realises that the book is not about the apostles it is about Jesus working through the apostles in his power. The power is always from God, the apostles simply serve as conduits for the power to come into the lives of those in need.

---

[63] Keith Warrington, *Healing and Suffering*, (Milton Keynes: Paternoster, 2005) 99; see also Petts, *Just a taste*.
[64] Warrington, *Healing*, 101, for a six-point summary of the important aspects of healings in Acts.

Acts 5:15-16 shows how the power of God working through the apostles was starting to be known throughout the area. F.F. Bruce comments:

> Even from outlying towns and villages of Judea people streamed into the capital with their sick folk in hope of profiting from the apostles' healing ministry.[65]

Notice the impact of these miracles, they brought a sense of 'awe' on believer and unbeliever alike (Acts 3:10). Therefore, we must look on the miraculous as a great aid to evangelism. This is so because the wonderful effects of the power of God on an individual who had a physical/mental problem allow the apostles to point the crowd to the Lord Jesus Christ.

The power-encounters as they are now labelled were a vital element in the life of the New Testament church (Acts 13:6-13; Acts 16:16-24; Acts 28:1-10). In each of these incidents, it was always the benefit of the individual delivered from demon possession or sickness that was paramount. In no place do the apostles promote themselves or their power it is always diverted to God this is recorded in Acts 14:8-18 where the people of Lystra granted divine status to Paul and Barnabas. The apostles immediately divert the attention from themselves to God. It is possible that individuals can become so taken up with their 'power' that they become the centre of attention and detract from the fact that it is God alone who provides the power for such acts. Beware the person who promotes their 'power' and 'spirituality' and takes the attention and does not give praise to God; humility is the watchword for people used by God.

Two very important passages must be mentioned in order to keep a balance in these matters: 2 Timothy 4:20 and 2 Corinthians 12:7-10. God does not always see fit to heal, the individual must submit to his will. Donald Gee writing on 2 Timothy 4:20 states:

> It may well be that in the bold statement that Paul left Trophimus sick at Miletam we have one of those intentional assertions of the Bible intended to keep us from extremes.[66]

The local church must be kept from extremes of thinking, teaching and practice balance in all things spiritual is imperative to the proper growth of the local

---

[65] F.F. Bruce, *Acts of the Apostles*, (Grand Rapids: Eerdmans, 1988) 109.
[66] Donald Gee, *Trophimus I Left Sick*, (London: Elim, 1952) 30.

church. The comments of James 5:14-18 must serve as a basis for the local church and its ministry in healing(s); here the divine standard is set, and it must be followed. James refers specifically to those who are too sick to get to a congregational gathering therefore the elders can be called for a home visit. I will also add that in the congregational gathering if a person requires prayer then the responsibility rests on the elders. However, in a church which does not recognise elders this could lead to misunderstanding; in such a case I suggest that church leaders should take the responsibility. Yet, throughout the NT Paul often calls on all people to pray for him and so we must not get too hung up on Elders alone praying for the sick in a public meeting.

Prayer is a universal ministry and if the heart is correct and the desire is for God to move through them then who should refuse people to pray! Luke-Acts does not establish or even hint at a healing methodology, however, those used in healing/miraculous must be aware of the significance of 1 Corinthians 12:8-11 and, that all power and authority come from the Lord Jesus, through the Spirit. If Acts emphasises anything it is the essential person and work of the Spirit in the life of the believer whether for healing, witnessing or simply living the Christian life. However, in respect to other miraculous interventions there is no set practice established in the biblical narrative; it is worthy of noting that faith is essential (Matthew 17:20) and being attuned to the divine will for any given situation is necessary (Matthew 6:10).

Think it Over!

What place should/does the miraculous play in the 21st century Church?

Is there a place for miraculous in modern society?

How does a leader manage the extremes of thinking and practice in a congregation?

Chapter 13

The Unwanted Blessing: Persecution

But Saul, still breathing out threats and murder against the disciples of the Lord, went to the high priest… Acts 9:1

Within the Christian life many prefer to focus on the positive side of experience however, there is a subject that is crucial to the life of the Christian which is often overlooked: persecution! This is not a pleasant subject but one which is relevant to the 21st century church; today there is much persecution in the world. Organisations such as Release International and Open Doors do much to promote the issue and call for government and church intervention in societies where persecution is a major problem. Persecution is an expected aspect of church life trouble has been guaranteed since the beginning of the church; the people of God have been persecuted throughout the biblical narrative. Israel was persecuted by neighbouring powers, Jesus was rejected and persecuted throughout his ministry and the early church suffered much persecution as recorded in Acts.

Persecution in the Gospel of Luke

Persecution could be labelled as "The Unwanted Blessing" (Matthew 5:10-12; Luke 6:22-36).

In his writing Luke is presenting a balanced overview of the life of the early Church and Christian experience and from the very beginning persecution is obvious Luke 2:34-35. Even the birth narratives are tinged with the promise of trouble ahead for both Jesus and his mother Mary.

This theme runs throughout the life of Jesus:

1. Spiritual opposition (Luke 4:1-11).
2. Human opposition (Luke 4:28-29).
3. Religious opposition (Luke 13:10-17; Luke 20:1-8).
4. Political opposition (Luke 23:1-12).

The fact that Jesus endured persecution for the sake of the greater impact of the gospel compels one to consider how important this message is to the world. Despite persecution the gospel had to be fully preached in the first century; God's plans for humanity's redemption had to culminate in the Cross and the empty tomb. The four areas of opposition as mentioned above are present in the 21st century world. Spiritual opposition is the major theme which could be said to be the root of the other three areas.

Paul, writing to Ephesus, instructs the church about the reality of spiritual opposition, where the opposition for the Christian as the spiritual realm (Ephesians 6:10-20). As Stott write: 'Beneath surface appearances an unseen spiritual battle is raging.'.[67] This raging battle is played out in the lives of people who are being torn between two possible ways of living: following Jesus or remaining estranged from the gospel. It is interesting to follow Stott's thinking on Ephesians 6:10-20, where he continues to suggest that the reality of the opposition is the devil, a figure known to his readers. This raise the question of whether the church today realises its opponent is real and powerful?

Stott continues to state the reason for Paul's engagement with this difficult topic of demonic opposition and cosmic powers and principalities: 'In any case, his purpose is not to satisfy our curiosity, but to warn us of their hostility and teach us how to overcome them'..[68] There is a necessity for the Christian to be very aware of the enemy he is a powerful if defeated foe however, there is always the possibility that if the defences are lowered disaster could result. As you face various opposition in your experience whether that be human, political or religious remember that the true battle is not with those who perpetrate such trouble but with the enemy who desires to see you fall from grace. This is why it is essential that the disciple of Jesus is one who as we stated in Part 1 is spiritually strong depending on the Lord for all power and support through life.

Jesus suffered persecution at the hands of 'ungodly men' subsequent generations have faced similar attacks many resulting in the martyrdom of faithful people intent on simply living for Jesus. Never forget those who are persecuted for righteousness sake especially if you live in a society which has religious freedom and where going to church is no more frowned upon than going to the gym. Please don't fall into the trap of thinking that'll never happen

---

[67] John Stott, *The Message of Ephesians*, (Leicester: IVP, 1979/1989) 261.
[68] Stott, *Ephesians*, 261.

here, the enemy is devious and powerful and when your guard is lowered, he can deal a terrible blow. Take refuge in the armour of God as listed in Ephesians 6:13-18, which is provided to ensure your spiritual survival and the advancement of the gospel remembering that prayer must accompany all the armour.

Persecution in Acts

Following the death of Jesus his resurrection and ascension the embryonic Church is left wondering about its future. Acts 2 introduces the Paraclete 'helper' in the form of the Spirit it is to be his role to empower, keep, guide and direct the Church Age. Peter's Pentecost sermon and the great results as seen in Acts 2:41 no doubt filled the disciples with hope and Acts 3 again illustrates great success at the Temple gate. However, within a very short space of time, the Church was being persecuted for its stance. John Stott writes:

> But almost immediately a perilous storm blew up, a storm of such ferocity that the church's very existence was threatened..[69]

Acts poses three major problems that the Church had to contend with which could lead to persecution:

1. A dead saviour. This would have been the view of many of the Jewish leaders as they would not believe that the Messiah would die. But he would be an all-conquering leader to deliver Israel from its Roman oppressors.
2. A new religious community. To some the early Christ's ones were simply an irritating sect within Judaism. They were led by largely uneducated men from the backwaters of Galilee and their spiritual head was a carpenter! Surely this was no way for anyone to follow God.
3. Gentile inclusion. To the Jews this would have been anathema; how dare anyone think that an unclean, pagan Gentile could worship alongside God-fearing Jews. It could also work the other way in that the Gentile converts could struggle to associate with Jewish converts who had been so exclusive in their old religion.

---

[69] John Stott, *The Message of Acts,* (Leicester: IVP, 1991), 88.

These three areas are important in understanding the cultural and religious context of the early NT. How can the hero die? This may have been the question asked by the devout Jews who saw their Messiah in the line of all conquering king David and not treated as a common criminal. Death and especially death by crucifixion was no way to begin the revolution that would 'restore the kingdom to Israel'; of course the people of the day looked for a political kingdom, liberation from Roman oppression and not a spiritual future kingdom which would be the home of peace and righteousness. A persecuted community! There had been enough persecution in the history of Israel none more so than the years of slavery spent in Egypt. Why or how could a new kingdom of God a new vision for humanity allow for a continuation of the persecution?

Liberty and freedom were the desire of the people of Israel how could they marry this new faith in a dead Messiah to a mixed bag of fishermen and tax collectors who were persecuted due to their new faith? Surely, God's people would be blessed, empowered and free to rule in his authority. Then finally Gentile inclusion. Probably the most shocking of all the problems raised by the new sect. God's people were the people of Abraham, the Gentiles were imposters, heathen and ungodly hence they had no part in God's kingdom. The devout Jewish people of the day could never accept Gentiles as receiving anything from the hand of God this is dealt with throughout the Luke-Acts narrative; Luke 2:10 'all people' are included in the initial announcement of salvation. In Luke 10:25-37 the Samaritan is held up as a person of virtue and integrity.

In Acts the Gentiles come more to the foreground;

> Simon the magician (a Samaritan) hears the gospel, others of Samaritan heritage also here the message (Acts 8:9-25);
> An Ethiopian receives the gospel (Acts 8:26-38);
> Acts 10 is a pivotal chapter in the change of emphasis to include the Gentiles in the evangelisation of the world. Peter's vision of the clean and unclean animals prepares the way for him to interact with Cornelius a Roman soldier. This occasion is sealed by the arrival of the Holy Spirit into the lives of the Gentile audience (Acts 10:44-48). God shows no partiality and race is no boundary to the salvation of God.

From Acts 13 the focus of the gospel becomes world-wide; no one nation stands out as being in more or less need of the gospel than any other. Paul and the other apostles accompanied by a variety of support workers and helpers set out on a campaign of gospel ministry reaching to the 'end of the earth'. As they go, they head into opposition, persecution, violence and death but still they go knowing the message is more important than personal security or well-being. What a great example the early pioneers of the faith set for 21st century disciples: are people today prepared to go and face the persecution for the sake of the greater good of those without Christ?

The book of Acts records almost immediate problems for the early believers:

1. verbal mocking, very often persecution begins with small matters (Acts 2:13).
2. physical persecution begins with the apostle being 'laid hands on' by the authorities and put in prison (Acts 4:1-3).
3. problems often originate from jealousy and ignorance on the part of the persecutor (Acts 4:13).
4. the law of the land can stand in the way of the gospel (Acts 4:15-22).
5. physical persecution can be hard (Acts 5:40).
6. we can pay the ultimate price (Acts 7:54–60).
7. the situation can become a national problem (Acts 8:1-3).
8. some people take great pleasure in causing problems (Acts 9:1-2).

The words of Jesus recorded in John 16:32-33 are again fulfilled in the pages of Acts. Persecution will come, but the Lord is in ultimate control of the Christians situation; no true work of God will go unopposed. It is essential that we remember the suffering of our Lord on Calvary when we consider our own suffering or persecution (Luke 23:33-49). The writer of Hebrews directs the reader to this very subject in Hebrews 12:1-4; yes, suffering may come but always keep Jesus and his suffering in your sight for this will bring you hope of ultimate deliverance.

Think it Over!

What is your response to possible persecution?

Do you experience persecution?

How should we react towards persecutors?

Chapter 14

I will Come Again: The Parousia.

This Jesus, who was taken up from you into heaven, will come in the same way as you saw him go into heaven. Acts 1:11

> History is going somewhere. It is not meaningless. It is not random. It is not eternal. There will be a real end just as there was a real beginning. And at the end we will find none other than Jesus Christ.[70]

These thoughts of Michael Green summarise the importance of engaging with the return or Second Coming of Jesus. This NT theme is introduced in Luke-Acts and developed throughout the NT epistles. It is a subject of much debate and disagreement however, it is vital to accept the reality of the Parousia or 'presence' of Jesus for a second time on earth. This belief underpins all the evangelistic efforts of the local Church and individual Christian: time is running out and there is an urgent message to proclaim. Luke-Acts pays significant attention to this doctrine however most of the information available on the subject is found within the teachings of Jesus in the Gospel. In Acts there is less emphasis upon the cause of evangelism and greater emphasis placed on the how of evangelism. However, it must be noted that the Parousia is the great backdrop against which the history and work of the Church is recorded.

The wider study of the return of Jesus comes within the area of Eschatology or the study of the eschaton or last days. This teaching was brought back into prominence through people such as John N. Darby (1800-1882) an important figure in the Brethren movement; C.I. Schofield (1843-1921), who invested much effort in the translation of a Bible with his theological emphasis. The Second Coming was popularised by the Pentecostal movement that began in the early 20th century.[71]

---

[70] Michael Green, *The Message of Matthew*, (Leicester: IVP, 1988/2000), 253.
[71] Marion Field, *John Nelson Darby Prophetic Pioneer*, (Godalming: Highland Books, 2008). Palmer, *Emergence*, 206-215.

The Pentecostals took the view that evangelism was an immediate necessity because Jesus could return at any moment and people simply needed to be ready. The conversation of Pentecostal evangelists, pastors and members revolved around a simple question; 'are you ready?' Their interpretation led to an emphasis on avoiding 'worldly' pursuits and pleasures for fear of being contaminated by sin and missing the return of Jesus or not being in a spiritually fit condition to enjoy an eternal reward. This was an aspect of their teaching on the pursuit of holiness, much of which centred on avoiding worldly attitudes and sins rather than focussing on a relationship with Jesus as the sanctifier of one's life.

Furthermore, the prospect of a 'mansion' in heaven caused many of the lower working classes to join the Pentecostals as they saw a future release from the hardships of industrial life, poverty and oppression.[72] 'Heaven is better than this' led to an expectant eschatology focussed on John 14:1-6, but also motivated a missionary spirit due to Acts 1:8-11 where the Spirit has come to empower witness because Jesus is coming again. It is of interest to question if the 21st century church has lost sight of this urgency and has become complacent in its mission and evangelistic endeavours. I suggest that this is the case particularly in the West where a more comfortable lifestyle and prosperous living standards have turned people's attention from the desire to be delivered from this world. However, there is a greater concern that people are so happy with life on earth they no longer desire to spend eternity with Jesus.

Even more concerning is a lack of desire to meet Jesus because their spiritual condition is poor resulting from a lack of understanding of the true work of the cross and the salvation acquired through that horrific event. I call Christian leaders to revisit the centrality of the cross, the impact of salvation and the hope of spending eternity with Jesus, and to preach and teach these subjects with greater passion. I call all disciples of Jesus to re-evaluate your understanding of Jesus, how much do you love him, and do you desire to see him and be with him for eternity. If you love someone you should want to be with them; do you love Jesus, and do you want to be with him?

---

[72] This was particularly true in the valleys of SE. Wales, UK where many people were engaged in the coal mining or steel making industries. Life was often cut short through sickness due to poor hygiene, epidemics, or work-related accidents, see Palmer, *Emergence*.

Views on the Parousia

The major theological positions on the Return of Christ are summarised in the following teachings:[73]

1. Amillennialism: Second Coming will initiate the eternal state.
2. Post-millennialism: Christ will return after the Millennium period.
3. Pre-millennialism: Christ will return before the Millennium.

These major views have been argued and debated over the centuries and all have their strengths and weaknesses. I recommend further study of this interesting topic. However, I would also suggest that it is vital not to get too bogged down in the details, arguments and counter arguments but simply embrace the fact that Jesus will return and allow that knowledge to motivate your pursuit of holiness and encourage greater evangelistic efforts. As Darrell Bock comments:

> We know in part now, and we make our case recognizing that we are trying our best to understand scripture within the limitations we now possess. One day we will know fully – and more importantly – be fully known (1 Corinthians 13:12). All of us look forward to that wonderful eternity in the beyond when we can rejoice in a unity about which now we can only dream.[74]

Eschatology in Luke-Acts

Luke's intention is to record the early history of the Christian church based on the work of Jesus through the apostles by the Spirit. His underlying theme is the centrality of Jesus and this is recognised in the need to preach the gospel until Jesus returns. However, as the details of Acts focusses on people at work for the gospel the reader can forget that it's about Jesus rather than the apostles. If the return of Jesus is re-emphasised in the local church, then the focus on the necessity for the church to be working towards that event will be more visible. If the church continues to focus on people and what they do rather than why they do it then the message has the potential to become people centred and not Christ centred. If this occurs it is likely that the means and methods replaces the

---

[73] Stanley N. Gundry (Ed), *Three Views on the Millennium and Beyond,* (Grand Rapids MI: Zondervan, 1999), for a fuller explanation of the major teachings.
[74] Darrell Bock, 'Summary Essay' in Gundry (Ed), *Three Views,* 309.

motive, all should be engaged in mission because time is running out, not because someone has a new idea to reach the lost, or a new speaker becomes the centre of attention. The missional approach to Christianity has much to offer and although I would not agree with all the principles of this approach there's much worth considering.[75]

Acts is not about Paul or Peter but about Jesus; your local church, your experience and ministry is not about you but about the centrality of Jesus, both on a local level but on a wider world stage with an eschatological impact. Furthermore, it is about how the Christian disciple or follower of Jesus introduces Jesus to the world, the church has spent too much time introducing people to church and forgetting it is Jesus who people need to meet. Are you a converser about Jesus and what he has done in your life or are you one who converses about the programme at your church, the church's renowned pastor, the size of the offering and the number of meetings you attend? Your response to this question will determine if you are living with the Parousia as a motivation for service. If the first century church was making an impact, I suggest it is because they believed they had a short time to

There are a few important issues to consider in respect to Luke's eschatology:

1. Jerusalem is at the centre of God's plans (Luke 9:22, 44-45, 51-56; Luke 18:31-34; Luke 19:28-44; Acts 1:9-11).
2. The 'last days' set the tone for Luke's evangelistic work (Acts 2:17).
3. Imminence has been replaced by an urgency for work (Luke 24:46-49.
4. Eschatological concepts underlie Luke's theology especially pneumatology (Acts 1:8-11).
5. Pneumatology depends on a 'last days' interpretation of the Church Age (Acts: 2:1-21).

Luke's Eschatology: A Summary Luke 21:5-38

Luke outlines his interpretation of end time events by recording the message of Jesus to the people of Jerusalem. Mention is made of:

1. False messiahs.
2. Political turmoil.

---

[75] Reggie McNeal, *Missional Renaissance*, (San Francisco: Jossey-Boss, 2009), Alan Roxburgh and Fred Romanuk, *The Missional Leader*, (San Francisco: Jossey-Boss, 2006).

3. Natural turmoil.
4. Distress of the nations.
5. Cosmic signs.
6. Persecution.
7. Parousia.

All of these 'signs' are precursors to the return of Jesus this has been viewed as God giving humanity plenty of warning about the climax of world history. Acts 1:11 is the promise of the heavenly being; Luke 24:49-53 and its fulfilment of the words of Jesus. There is also John 14:3; Acts 2:41, 47 and Acts 6:7.

Albert Barnes commenting on Acts 1:11 says:

> We are in these verses presented with the most grand and wonderful events that this world has ever known – the ascension and return of the Lord Jesus. Here is consolation for the Christian; and here is a source of ceaseless alarm to the sinner.[76]

The Second Coming of Christ is seen to be the 'hope' of all believers, as it provides the prospect of one day seeing the Lord Jesus and spending eternity with him. The Apostle Paul writes about the hope of the believer in a number of his epistles and calls his readers to look forward to the event with eager anticipation.

The Second Coming is both a hope and a warning:

Hope:

Titus 1:2 eternal life.
Titus 2:13 seeing the Lord.
Titus 3:7 eternal life.

Warning:

The bad situation in 2 Peter 3:1-11.

v9 - the promise will come about.
v10 - a sudden event.
v11 - warning about how we live.

---

[76] Albert Barnes, *The Acts of the Apostles*, (London: Blackie and Sons, n.d.), 16.

If all are to come to repentance then the gospel must be presented in the light of the Second Coming, warning people about the eternal consequences. (See Matthew 25:13; Luke 12:40; Mark. 14:62; 1 Corinthians 15:51-55; Revelation 21:4-5).

The apostles preached the gospel in the light of the fact that their Lord was coming again. This caused them to have a sense of urgency about their work and especially evangelism. How long would they have to preach the gospel before He returned (Romans 13:11)? This is an interesting question especially as the gospel is still being presented in the 21st century. However, despite the time lapse the message is still the same and the gospel must still be presented in every generation as if it were the last.

Living out the gospel considering the second coming is a message recorded by Paul in his Thessalonian correspondence. This aspect of basic Christian living is dealt with especially in 1 Thessalonians 4-5.[77] As Paul brings 1 Thessalonians to a conclusion he focuses attention on this vital aspect of the Christians experience; the future and he engages with the true reason behind his concerns over salvation, leadership, growth and conduct which he has dealt with in the previous chapters. People spend a lot of time and effort in planning for our future yet others who are more fatalistic approach situations with the phrase 'well that's simply my destiny'. But what is our true destiny? Where are we going in this life & what is its purpose. Well Paul helps us by providing one verse that highlights the true destiny for our lives in light of what God thinks about everything (1 Thessalonians 5:9). A few simple thoughts on this central chapter as I bring this section to a conclusion.

1. The first major issue to be aware of is the reality of the return of Jesus (1 Thessalonians 4:13-5:8). The Thessalonians had become concerned with the end of the world and rightly so, but their concern had led them to a place of questioning the events that will surround this end. Paul gives them some comfort and encouragement by stating the reality of the event (Thessalonians 4:16-17; 5:2-3). Yes, this will happen, the end will come, Jesus will return. However, all is in the control of God and they should not worry about the details but focus on the big picture of their being prepared for the climactic events. The parable of

[77] John MacArthur, *1 & 2 Thessalonians* (Chicago: Moody, 2002). Leon Morris, *1 and 2 Thessalonians* (Leicester: IVP, 1984).

the wise and foolish virgins provides insight into this essential aspect (Matthew 25:1-13). This position on the reality of the return is consistent with the teaching of scripture; the context of our ultimate destiny is the return of Christ (Matthew 24:42; John 14:3; Acts 1:11; 2 Peter 3:1-13). Paul is concerned that all his readers are aware of the future and that there is more to life than meets the eye; there is a future state for which we must all be prepared.

2. Secondly, he makes them aware of the reality of the hope contained in the end time events (1 Thessalonians 4:13). Here Paul is speaking of the expectations or confidence people can have in life and death. The reality of life is that there are two possible conditions hopelessness or hopefulness this is emphasised in Ephesians 2:12. Hope is something that depends on our relationship with God if you are without God you have no hope! But hope of what? Being brought near to God in a relationship with him through Christ who died for us (John 14:1-6; Ephesians 2:13, 18-19). Many people hope for things in this life, but the reality of true hope focuses on what we know and expect from God. What are you expecting today? What are you hoping for today?

In this life it may be some earthly or physical comfort but in 2 Corinthians 4:16-18, Paul puts everything in life into an eternal perspective; our perceived difficulties are nothing in light of what God has in store for those who trust him (Romans 8:18). The Thessalonians were worried about those who had died and Paul says not to focus on the negatives of this life but on the reality of the hope founded in God through Christ. Those who have died will not miss out on the eternal state as all is in God's hands and not in the hands of human leaders, apostles, pastors or preachers.

3. The final aspect dealt with by Paul is the reality of eternity (1 Thessalonians 4:17). Paul finishes off this chapter and commences the next with this wonderful assurance of the reality of eternity when he says we will *always be with the Lord*. Paul's concern for the Thessalonians is that their worries over those who had died was affecting how they lived, but he assures them that the reality is that God, in Christ, deals in eternal matters and not simply those of this world. There is more to life than what you have; there is more to be expected than physical death; there is an eternity to face and be prepared for. The analogies are always comforting; to be home or in

the place of comfort (2 Corinthians 5:6-8); a *'better'* place (Philippians 1:23); true life comes through Christ and it culminates in *'glory'* (Colossians 3:4). In the 21st century people have lost sight or interest in eternity, both inside and outside the church. Sadly, the majority wander through life with no prospects, no eternal perspective and no thought of life after death. This leads to a lack of desire to prepare for eternity, even in the church a 'ticket to heaven' attitude is prominent and hence eases the pressure of urgency in evangelising. People are content with their 'ticket' and get on with life with little or no thought of the consequences of neglecting presenting the message to others. Paul calls his readers to be aware of eternity. God is an eternal being who deals in eternal matters; people have eternal souls which require care, attention and preparation for eternity. Today it is essential to regain this eternal perspective within the local Christian community as this will motivate mission and evangelism.

1 Thessalonians 4-5 serves as a good conclusion to this look at the theological themes of Luke-Acts as it places everything into the perspective of the return of Christ. Paul informs the Thessalonians and subsequent readers; that all need to know they do not live in a little bubble but have an eternity to face. This is emphasised by the fact that the Lord Jesus Christ desires a people who are pure and who will enjoy his eternal rewards with whom he can share his eternal glory and inheritance (1 Thessalonians 5:5-9). So, the question to leave with you as this look at Luke-Acts draws to a close is:

Are you a true disciple of Jesus acting out your faith which has the end goal of witnessing to him as the eternal God and saviour of the world?

Think it Over!

Do you believe in the Second Coming of Jesus?

Parousia delayed how do you preach/teach the imminence of the event?

How focussed is your ministry on eschatological principles?

How does the Church, an eschatological community, relate to the world?

Chapter 15

Here, There and Everywhere: World Mission

Thus it is written, that the Christ should suffer and on the third day rise from the dead, and that repentance for the forgiveness of sins should be proclaimed in his name to all nations… Luke 24:46-47

'*All nations'* is the key to understanding Lukan missiology. For Luke the mission of Jesus through his church is to the whole world and not limited to Israel. Mission and evangelisation are central themes in the Bible and especially for Luke-Acts. Mission or evangelisation commences with the announcement of the birth of Jesus (Luke 1:26-38) and continues to Acts 28 where Paul is left preaching and teaching in Rome. Mission is allied to the arrival of the Holy Spirit, this avenue of Christian service affects the individual and the community both Christian and non-Christian.

This area of service is essential to the on-going growth of the Christian community, and the church cannot rest on its laurels but must be proactive in its engagement with mission and evangelisation. It is necessary for the church to move away from an attitude that it exists for the members that is to simply provide spiritual refreshment, encouragement and emotional support for the congregation. This is an important aspect of church life however, its lifeblood is mission, and it must reach out and seek to enlarge its spiritual footprint in the community. If the church neglects mission it is neglecting its primary purpose of reaching the nations for Christ.

The Requirement of Mission

As Luke is particularly interested in the eschatological Spirit, the key issue is the link with mission (Luke 24:46-49 and Acts 1:8). The themes of mission is represented in the life and ministry of Jesus which is the 'blueprint' or example for the succeeding generations of his followers; all are called to preach the gospel. Almost the whole of the second section of Acts, chapters 9-28, is devoted to Paul the Missionary.

George Peters suggests that mission is the very heartbeat of the Christian community when he writes:

> We are moving in the centre stream of the New Testament when I assert that the principal task of the Church is to communicate intelligibly and effectively a divine message to the world in order to bring man to a living relationship with Christ by faith.[78]

This assertion by Peters, reveals the true calling of all Christian believers, i.e. that they should be involved in evangelisation and the communication of the Gospel. This task was entered upon positively, powerfully and prayerfully by the embryonic Christian community as recorded in Acts. A community that took its lead from the example of Jesus and the twelve as seen in the Gospel of Luke. Jesus came to preach the gospel and left the disciples with the mandate to continue its proclamation. The message and experience they had received thrust them out into the field of Christian witness/evangelism/mission. What greater task was entrusted to the new community and is so today, than its expansion? The fire of Christian mission that was ignited in Luke-Acts has burned over successive centuries since Peter preached that first evangelistic sermon on the Day of Pentecost.

Mission Issues in Luke

1. Jesus introduces a new standard for mission; the gospel (Luke 4:18-19).
2. The twelve are the first missionary team (Luke 5:1-11; Luke 9:1-6).
3. The seventy can be viewed as illustrating embryonic church-wide mission (Luke 10:1-29).

Here it is possible to see how Luke sets the scene for the future of Christian mission, in that it is no longer the sole possession of the spiritual leaders or elite but is a command for all to follow. Hence for Luke, the Spirit is a requirement in order to assist natural people with the supernatural work.

---

[78] George Peters, *A Biblical Theology of Mission*, (Chicago: Moody Press, 1972), 209; see also Howard Peskett & Vinoth Ramachandra, *The Message of Mission*, (Leicester: IVP, 2003); A. Scott Moreau (Ed), *Introducing World Mission*, (Grand Rapids: Baker, 2005).

The Message of Mission in Luke-Acts

The kerygma or message proclaimed that is the message of mission is vital in our understanding of Luke's view of mission[79]. This message develops throughout the Luke-Acts narrative, today it is necessary for the church to reassess what message is being proclaimed from its pulpits and in the streets. Is the message the full gospel as found and developed in the practice and preaching of the early church?

The Content of the Message of Mission

The Lukan perspective on mission allows the student to understand something of his Christology which must be the centre of the gospel message. Jesus is portrayed in a variety of important roles. He is viewed as:

1. The Son of Man. an eschatological title. that traces the heritage of Jesus to Adam emphasises the humanity of Christ (Luke 3:23-38).
2. The Son of the Most High emphasises his divinity (Luke 1:32).
3. He is eternal (Luke 1:33).
4. He is the saviour (Luke 9:56; Luke 19:10).
5. He suffers and dies (Luke 22:39-46; Luke 23:33-45).
6. He is the Risen and Ascended Lord (Luke 24:6; Acts 1:9; Acts 2:22-24).
7. He is the provider of the Spirit (Luke 24:49; Acts 2:33).
8. He is the anticipated returning King (Luke 17:22-37; Acts 1:11).

As the early Church began its existence it needed to be assured of its foundations as the sermons in Acts illustrate everything centres on Jesus, his life, ministry, death, resurrection, ascension and return. This is imperative to the on-going ministry of the local church in the 21st century; Jesus must be central it's all about him and the message of salvation offered through the gospel. Consideration must be given not only to the programme of mission in the church but also to the content of the message promoted by the church. A well-structured programme will not bring true conversions unless the content of the message is biblical and powerfully presented. Luke also reminds his readers that the spectacular is not the purpose of mission (Luke 10:17-20). This incident challenges the disciples to 'keep their feet on the ground' even amongst the thrilling supernatural occurrences; it's not the spectacular that matters but simply that their names are known to God. Salvation must be the driving force

---

[79] I dealt more fully with the kerygma in a previous chapter.

of all mission and evangelisation everything else is subsidiary even though very beneficial to those recipients of God's grace.

Mission in Acts

Acts begins with a focus on the necessary power for mission which follows the instruction by Jesus about the basic principles of the Kingdom of God(Acts 1:8). Luke portrays mission for the embryonic church as:

1. A power encounter in the spiritual realm (Acts 1:8).
2. A universal undertaking (Acts 10:34-48).
3. A message centred solely on Jesus (Acts 4:12).
4. A divine command (Acts 4:18-20).
5. A presentation of salvation through repentance and faith (Acts 2:38; Acts 3:19).

The Proclamation

The church is left on earth in order to proclaim the gospel in mission through the power of the Spirit; the church then is:

1. The guardian of the message.
2. The transmitter of the message.

As such there is a duty of responsibility placed upon the local church to remain as the body which maintains the truth. Paul reminds Timothy of this aspect of churches existence, it is the edifice that should promote and maintain the truth and that truth is expressed in the following verse (1 Timothy 3:15).[80] The truth centres on Jesus and his ministry on earth and on-going heavenly ministry; is that the focus of the local church you attend, is truth at its heart, is the gospel the motivating factor for the existence of the local church? This may require a shift in mind-set for what some people believe to be the role and purpose of the church; the liberal thinking that has seen churches relegated to social centres, social clubs or charity outlets detracts from its true purpose: promoting life changing encounters with God. This is not to say that charitable good works are not necessary but beware that they do not take over the programme so that it becomes natural and not spiritual. The centrality of the message cannot be

---

[80] Donald Guthrie, *The Pastoral Epistles*, (Leicester: IVP, 1990). Philip H. Towner, *The Letters to Timothy and Titus*, (Cambridge: Eerdmans, 2006).

overstated in the life, plans, programmes and achievements of the local church. Be gospel centred and a group that proclaims that divine message of hope and reconciliation.

The Importance of the Sermons in Acts

The primary means of transmitting the message in Acts is through sermons, I dealt at more length with this in the previous section on the word of God. Luke records a few sermons of the apostles Peter and Paul these aid our understanding of the focus of the message in the early church[81].

In Acts 2:14, Peter's first reaction to the crowd was to preach the gospel. This sermon is based on OT passages, it relates to the people how God moved and worked in Jewish history, culminating in the presentation of Jesus the suffering Messiah and the one raised from the dead in victory. There is hope, warning, detail of the rejection of Christ, the role of the Spirit and the example of the life and ministry of Jesus. As you sit and regularly listen to sermons are, they hype, personal motivation to a successful life, philosophical debate, self-improvement, man-made ideas or are they biblically grounded and focussing on Jesus?

Acts 3:1-26 sees Peter and John giving God the glory for the healing of the lame man. This man was expecting the usual however, when God's people are involved the unexpected should be the expected. Peter and John, following this miracle of healing, testify not to their own power or ability but to God's gracious dealings with the lame man. Peter preaching is grounded in the OT narrative and urges his audience to repentance and faith in Jesus.

In Acts 7:2-53, Stephens defence is an evangelistic sermon. How God can work even in the direst situations. This sermon when unpacked reveals an OT basis for all the events surrounding the life and death of Jesus. This sermon further illustrates how the true gospel should produce a reaction, even if negative, from its hearers. How do people react to the message presented through your local church? If there is no reaction either positive or negative, I would question the content and purpose behind the message.

Acts 8 records the work of Philip the Evangelist, working in Samaria and in the wilderness preaching on both occasions. His preaching brought results many

---

[81] I dealt with the Speeches in Acts in an earlier chapter.

people were helped and converted though his preaching. Philip according to Acts 8:4-5 preached the word about Jesus. This is best illustrated in Acts 8:26-38 where his text was Isaiah 53, all of which points to Jesus the suffering Messiah. Never neglect the OT in the presentation of the new covenant for God was at work through Israel to bring the saviour to central focus.

Acts 17:16-34 illustrates Paul skill in the presentation of the word of God by using everyday situations and by using popular philosophy or poets to help bring his point to the hearers. Paul here reveals an interesting necessity, preachers should be aware of the social, cultural context in which they minister as this can help people interact with the message as it becomes culturally relevant. Contextualisation is a key element of gospel presentation; it is vital to be contextually relevant to your hearers.

However, it is important to note that Paul did not use the popular philosophers as his text but simply to illustrate and lead people forward into the truth of the gospel. Again, it is essential to note the reaction caused from the preached word; sarcasm, further inquiry and complete acceptance the full range of reactions possible from both 1st and 21st century populations. Take courage in mission and evangelisation there will rarely be widespread acceptance of the message however, because of the few that respond positively it is essential to keep sowing the seed of the word of God.

Acts 20:17-38 is a sermon with a difference; encouragement, warning and teaching to the church. Mission is only as good as the follow up teaching received by the converts. Sermons were a means of proclaiming the basic elements of the new faith centred on Jesus for the reason of seeing people turned from their old religion and brought into the Kingdom of God. In order to preach in a biblical manner, one must know the simple truths of the scriptures and be able to present them in a coherent manner.

Following on from evangelistic preaching the 'full gospel' relates to the everyday lifestyle of the disciple, here Paul addresses the elders in Ephesus warning them of the possible perils that can confront the congregation. Paul again bases his ministry on the word of God (Acts 20:20&27); the life of Jesus is central to the message (Acts 20:21); then the warning to watch out for false teachers who have only their own interests at heart (Acts 20:28-33). Verse 29 is particularly graphic in describing the horrific way false teachers should be understood; they are compared to wolves set on destroying and consuming helpless sheep. The leaders are to stand guard over the 'sheep' and provide spiritual protection form any outside troublemakers and those intent on destruction.

The sermons in Acts present a development in the theological thinking of the embryonic church; from a raw experience in Acts 2 of evangelistic Spirit empowered message, to the more rounded and fuller concerns of Paul as in Acts 20. Furthermore, it has to be recognised that all of these sermons were rooted in the OT narrative and the life experience of Jesus. If evangelism and mission is to be successful in the 21st century its message must be rooted in the word of God and centre on Jesus. For as Luke reminds his readers in Acts 1:1 it is all about Jesus.

Luke desires to portray a picture of the beginnings of the mission of the church; this mission is to be charismatic, reaching the world through the structure of the church and based upon the life, ministry, death, resurrection and return of Jesus. Soteriology is the essence of mission for Luke-Acts; salvation is the central theme and purpose of the church.

In the 21st century this vision for mission must be rekindled, the church, especially in the west, is struggling with the effects of a secular society and the only answer is to engage in vibrant evangelistic outreach that meets people at the point of their need. Every situation is unique, and we must be careful not to employ a 'one size fits all' policy for mission. It may be necessary for leaders in local churches to establish a working group for evangelism in the church, this group can then focus attention on the needs of the community and see where the church can interact most effectively with that wider society.

Do not be afraid of doing something different it is possible that past initiatives need to be revived or rejected, God may want to do a new thing among his people to impact the wider society. Do not fear change if it is in the will of God to progress the Kingdom on earth then the congregation should embrace it with open arms. However, never change the message but be flexible with the means by which the message is presented.

Think it Over!

What role does mission play in the life of the local church?

Do you personally and corporately support worldwide mission?

Consider how you heard the gospel; do you need to be more involved in promoting the faith?

Is the gospel always central to your ministry/mission?

Thoughts

This section has unearthed some of those practical and spiritual aspects of 'Acting out your Christianity.' They are all essentials that the disciple and the local church should consider and assess how or if they are an important part of the things they do in worship and service. Balance is so important in spiritual issues and no one area of theological or practical teaching should be either over emphasised or neglected, if this occurs then the edifice is constructed on uneven foundations and is liable to collapse. If you think prayer is important but organisation does not matter, then it may be time for you to reconsider the biblical standards and reassess if your thinking is in line with the Bible.

Part 3
Acts Today

Chapter 16

Where Now: Luke-Acts Today!

And welcomed all who came to him, proclaiming the kingdom of God and teaching about the Lord Jesus Christ with all boldness and without hindrance. Acts 28:30-31

It may be rather clichéd but the traditional, if a little romantic, view of the ending of Acts leaving the reader with an example from the apostle; whatever your situation (Paul was a prisoner) keep proclaiming the gospel. 'Acting Out Your Christianity' is a possible title for an 'Acts 29' style of vital faith which focusses not on the end of the life of the apostle Paul but on the driving force of his life, preaching the gospel. For whatever Paul faced at the hands of the Roman officials in the capital of the Empire, his deepest desire was to proclaim Christ, *'woe to me if I do not preach the gospel'* (1 Corinthians 9:16). This should be the driving force of every disciple of Jesus; keep preaching the gospel.

As we review the writings of Luke-Acts and the major themes found in its pages a brief summary of each major theme is required. For, this will allow the reader to reassess their position in relation to the image, example and action of a vital missional church.

Part 1 was an introduction to the technical issues of Luke-Acts. These may not be overly important to you however. Every disciple of Jesus should be familiar with the basic structure, purpose and teachings of the biblical narrative. Not all will be professors of hermeneutics or Bible historians, but a general knowledge of the biblical genres will enhance everyone's reading and understanding. If you can, I recommend you invest in a Bible Dictionary and make yourself familiar with the background and themes of the biblical writers and their writings.[82]

Part 2 highlighted the centrality of the Bible, prayer and the Holy Spirit. This emphasis on the spiritual foundations of the faith is one that requires

---

[82] I recommend a general volume like *The New Bible Dictionary* (Leicester: IVP, 1996) and Fee and Stuart, *How to Read the Bible;* there is also a plethora of online and electronic material available e.g. www.e-Sword.com

reintroduction to the 21st century Christian community. Without this solid foundation there is no hope of the individual disciple or the corporate body of Christ making progress and impacting the world for the gospel. Take a little time to consider your relationship to these major necessities in the life of the disciple of Christ. Acting out your Christianity can only be effective when based on the word of God, prayer and the power of the Spirit.

Do you read the word of God on a regular and systematic basis?

Do you pray, seriously seeking God to reveal his will for the situations you face daily?

Are you open to the leading, guiding and power of the Holy Spirit, your helper in life?

An examination of the Christian community in action was introduced with the subjects of unity, fellowship, water-baptism, breaking of bread (The Lord's Supper) and organisation. This allowed the reader to consider some of the more practical things that you can 'control'. Often people forget that they can impact the effectiveness of the local Christian community by their attitudes and actions. There should be a striving after unity in the hearts, lives and attitudes of every disciple; this is an often-neglected biblical principle to which people generally pay lip-service alone.

Saying the church is united simply because it meets together on a Sunday often belies the tensions lying just beneath the surface. Work at unity, seek out those with whom you have difficulties and endeavour to sort through your differences; you may be holding back the effectiveness of the gospel. Fellowship is no optional extra; there is a growing emphasis on the acceptability to dismantle the church programmes and focus on an individualistic expression of faith. Not being in fellowship with a local Christian community is unbiblical, separation from the local church should not be encourage as this will lead to isolation and hamper spiritual growth. The divine standard from the beginning was for fellowship; Adam, Eve and God fellowshipped in the garden; Israel was a called-out nation of people with set standards of living and worship. The NT introduces a disparate group of men known as the disciples who followed Jesus together. The development in Acts is of a variety of 'church' groups forming around a central faith. Hebrews calls people not to neglect meeting together, as is the habit of some (Hebrews 10:25). Then the final words of revelation of Jesus is given to seven churches in Asia, nowhere is the command to corporate fellowship rescinded.

I accept it may be necessary to adapt some aspects of the programmes of the church, however, never lose sight of the necessity of corporate fellowship which centres on the Lord Jesus Christ and the gospel.

Water baptism and breaking of bread are the two major ordinances of the church; they have a variety of interpretations which have been argued over for centuries. I simply want to encourage everyone to consider their place in your experience. Do they matter to you? Are they an important part of your experience? Will you consider water baptism and a regular observance of the Lord's Table in your church community? This will enhance your spirituality and deepen your relationship with Jesus.

Organisation is often the 'Cinderella' of the church. People are more interested in the music, preaching and social activity than in ensuring the church is correctly organised and biblically led.[83] There is a need of biblical organisation and spiritual leadership in the church it is not sufficient to say; 'we leave it to the Spirit to move'. God has given each person a brain and common sense by which biblical models can be examined and implemented in the local setting. As a member or leader of a local congregation can you please take the time to organise the programmes and purposes of the church so that the church is not looked at as a shoddy example of workmanship. I believe that the church should operate efficiently and with excellence in every department and be a shining example of efficiency.

Continuing the theme of the Christian community in action, four very important theological areas that enhance Acting Out your Christianity are; Miraculous, Persecution, Parousia, and Mission. These areas are inter-related and are prominent in the forefront of gospel impact.

Mission is the heartbeat of the disciple and the church; without mission the body ceases to grow and becomes a stagnant relic to historic religion this will eventually result in death. The mission of God through his church must be continued by every disciple. It is imperative that the church moves away from a belief that mission is only carried out by missionaries called to leave home for some distant land. Ephesians 4:11-13 highlights how all in the body of Christ are being fitted out to be involved in the *'work of ministry'* and building up the body. The word 'ministry' is diakonia which should be translated as service; hence the

---

[83] Palmer, *Essential Christian*; John Maxwell, *21 Indispensable Qualities of a Leader*, (Nashville, Thomas Nelson, 2012).

thought of someone being in the 'ministry' i.e. as a professional career, has detracted from the emphasis which should be placed on 'body ministry'. If everyone whatever their position in the local church purely saw themselves as servants then more work would be done, more results achieved, and a greater impact made or the gospel. A title/position driven church will not be as effective as a servant-based church in which every member is active in mission, reaching out to others in their particular situations.

The *miraculous* is a biblical principle that exhilarates some; concerns some; intrigues some; confuses some and enrages others. However, I believe that God is a God of the miraculous the biblical narrative records many instances of God's miraculous intervention in the life of his people, and for that matter those outside the chosen people. Why, if God worked like that in the past and the Holy Spirit records it for our benefit, do people doubt God can work in a similar manner today? It is though important to recognise that miracles do not happen simply for the person involved to be lauded as some super-spiritual being who can control the divine and cause the spectacular. Miracles occur to bring glory to God and serve the purpose of introducing people to the power of God to save and change lives.

As Jesus walked the earth or as the apostles toured the ancient Mediterranean world, the miracles performed opened up avenues to preach the gospel. If you believe in the miraculous why do you see it as necessary? If you disbelieve the miraculous why do you doubt that God can work in such ways to bring glory to his name? The church needs to re-visit the miraculous power of God and have a sensible, biblical understanding of why and how God can work in such amazing ways.

Nobody enjoys *persecution* and suffering yet the NT and especially Luke-Acts highlights this essential aspect of Christian service. The people of God have suffered persecution form their earliest times. In the 21st century this pattern of persecution continues and will until Jesus comes again. It must be the goal of the church not to ignore or do away with issues of persecution but to stay close to God to survive the various threats, insults, wounds and attacks of the enemy. Ephesians 6:10-20 provides a framework to stand firm in the faith and combat the opposition which can arise from many different directions. If you have never endured persecution then thank God and pray for those who are constantly in the 'line of fire', uphold such persecuted disciples in prayer and support them in any way you can so they know they are not alone in the fight. Also prepare yourself for the possibility of persecution; I often think the church in the west is not persecuted because it has lost its zeal for Jesus and is ineffective and therefore not a threat to the kingdom of darkness. If western Christianity regains its passion for Jesus and the lost then persecution will arise; but do not allow this to be a disincentive to seeking God and his blessing in the ministries he has called you to provide.

The whole of the biblical narrative is looking forward to one great event the return of Jesus – the *Parousia*. This will be the climax of God's dealings with this world and humanity. This should serve as motivation to Act Out Your Christianity; there's a reason for all this activity. It is to produce a church which is ready to be received by Jesus Christ at his return. The church does not work in vain or for no reason; its purpose is to see people brought out of darkness into the light before Jesus comes again. Working to a deadline is the underlying principle of Christian service. As you close this book and consider its impact remember one essential issue; time is running out and you have the answer to people's dilemmas Jesus Christ and him, crucified.

Are you 'Acting out your Christianity' or are you simply a Sunday pew filler who enjoys the entertainment of a service but has no intention of allowing the Bible to impact you on a personal level? A level at which your whole life is changed, perspectives altered, desires changed, hope renewed and purpose refocussed. I believe that a serious study of Luke-Acts will have a such a revolutionary effect on the disciple that the church will once again have the title of those 'who have turned the world upside down'.

Bibliography

Commentaries:

Barnes, Albert. *The Acts of the Apostles*. London: Blackie & Son n.d.

Bruce, F.F. *The Book of Acts*. Grand Rapids: Eerdmans, 1988.

Calvin, John. *Acts*. Nottingham: Crossway, 1995.

Carson, D.A. *The Gospel of John*. Apollos, 1991.

Fortner, Donald S. *Life after Pentecost*. Darlington: Evangelical Press, 1995.

Green, Michael. *30 Years That Changed the World*. Leicester: IVP, 1993; 2002.

Green, Michael. *The Message of Matthew*. Leicester: IVP, 1988; 2000.

Guthrie, Donald. *The Pastoral Epistles*. Leicester: IVP, 1990.

Haenchen, Ernst. *The Acts of the Apostles*. Oxford: OUP, 1971.

MacArthur, John. *1 & 2 Thessalonians*. Chicago: Moody, 2002

Marshall, I. Howard. *Acts*. Nottingham: IVP, 1980; 2008.

Morris, Leon. *1 and 2 Thessalonians*. Leicester: IVP, 1984.

Morris, Leon. *Luke*. Leicester: IVP, 1974/1984.

Pervo, Richard I. *The Gospel of Luke*. Salem, OR: Polebridge Press, 2014.

Peterson, David G. *The Acts of the Apostles*. Grand Rapids: Eerdmans, 2009 & Nottingham, Apollos, 2009.

Stott, John R.W. *The Message of Acts*. Leicester: IVP, 1998.

Stott, John. *The Message of Ephesians*. Leicester: IVP, 1979/1989.

Towner, Philip H. *The Letters to Timothy and Titus*. Cambridge: Eerdmans, 2006.

Wagner, C. Peter. *Acts of the Holy Spirit*. Ventura CA: Regal, 1994; 1995; 2000.

Wilcock, Michael. *The Message of Luke*. Leicester: IVP, 1979; 1997.

Historical & General:

Beasley-Murray, Paul. *Dynamic Leadership*. Eastbourne: MARC, 1990.

Berkhof, Louis. *Systematic Theology*. Edinburgh: Banner of Truth, 1998.

Berkouwer, C.G. *The Church*. Grand Rapids: Eerdmans, 1976.

Bock, Darrell L. *A Theology of Luke and Acts*. Grand Rapids: Zondervan, 2012

Bolt, Peter. *The Gospel to the Nations*. California: Apollos, 2002.

Bosch, David. *Transforming Mission*. Maryknoll: Orbis, 1991.

Brand, Chad (Ed.). *Perspectives on Spirit Baptism*. Nashville TN: B&H Publishing, 2004.

Brown, Paul E. *The Holy Spirit & The Bible*. Fearn: Christian Focus, 2002.

Bruce, F.F. *The Books and the Parchments*. London: Pickering, 1950

Bruner, F.D. *A Theology of the Holy Spirit*. Hodder & Stoughton, 1971.

Caird, G.B. *The Apostolic Age*. London: Duckworth, 1962.

Conzelmann, Hans. *The Theology of Saint Luke*. London: Faber, 1961.

Dunn, James D.G. *The Baptism in the Holy Spirit*. London: SCM, 1970.

Elwell, Walter A. (ed.). *Evangelical Dictionary of Biblical Theology*. Grand Rapids: Baker Books, 1996.

Fee, Gordon. *God's Empowering Presence*. Peabody, MA: Hendrickson, 1999.

Fee, Gordon D. and Douglas Stuart. *How to Read the Bible for all its Worth*. Bletchley: Scripture Union, 1994.

Field, Marion. John Nelson Darby. *Prophetic Pioneer*. Godalming: Highland Books, 2008

Gee, Donald. *Trophimus I Left Sick*. London: Elim, 1952.

Goldsworthy, Graeme. *According to Plan*. Leicester: IVP, 2002.

Grudem, Wayne. *Systematic Theology*. Leicester: IVP, 1994.

Grudem, Wayne (Ed). *Are Miraculous Gifts For Today?* Grand Rapids: Zondervan, 1996.

Gundry, Stanley (ed). *Three Views of the Millennium and Beyond*. Grand Rapids: Zondervan, 1999.

Guthrie, Donald. *New Testament Introduction*. Leicester: IVP, 1970.

Guthrie, Donald. *New Testament Theology*. Leicester: IVP, 1981.

Hodge, A.A. *Evangelical Theology*. Edinburgh: Banner of Truth, n.d.

Hollenweger, Walter J. *The Pentecostals*. London: SCM, 1976.

Hudson, Neil. *Imagine Church: Releasing Whole-Life Disciples*. Nottingham: IVP, 2012.

Karkkainen, Veli-Matti. *An Introduction to Ecclesiology*. Leicester: IVP, 2002.

Karkkainen, Veli-Matti. An Introduction to Pneumatology. Grand Rapids: Baker, 2002.

Keller, Tim. Preaching, London: Hodder and Stoughton, 2017.

Kydd, Ronald. Charismatic Gifts in the Early Church. Peabody: Hendrickson, 1984.

Lloyd-Jones, D. Martyn. Preachers and Preaching. London: Hodder and Stoughton, 1971.

Lord, Andrew. *Spirit Shaped Mission*. Milton Keynes: Paternoster, 2005.

McNeal, Reggie. *Missional Renaissance*. San Francisco: Jossey-Boss, 2009.

Marshall, I. Howard. *Luke - Historian and Theologian*. Exeter: Paternoster, 1970/1979.

Maxwell, John C. *The 21 Indispensable Qualities of a Leader*. Nashville TN.: Thomas Nelson, 1993.

Metzeger, Bruce. *The New Testament – Background, Growth and Content*. London: Lutterworth, 1969.

Moreau, A. Scott (Ed), *Introducing World Mission*. Grand Rapids: Baker, 2005.

Moule, C.F.D. *The Birth of the New Testament*. London: Black, 1981.

Palmer, Chris. *Essential Christian Leadership*. Pontypool: Faithbuilders, 2019.

Palmer, Chris. *The Emergence of Pentecostalism in Wales*. London: Apostolos, 2016.

Palmer, Chris. *The Pastoral Epistles: A Course Study in Pastoral Theology*. London: Faithbuilders, 2015.

Penney, John Michael. *The Missionary Emphasis of Lukan Pneumatology*. Sheffield: Sheffield Academic Press, 1997.

Peskett, Howard and Vinoth Ramachandra. *The Message of Mission*. Leicester: IVP, 2003.

Peters, George W. *A Biblical Theology of Missions*. Chicago: Moody Press, 1984.

Petts, David. *Just a Taste of Heaven*. Mattersey: Mattersey Hall, 2006.

Petts, David. *Body Builders: Gifts to Make your Church Grow*. Mattersey: Mattersey Hall, 2002.

Petts, David. *The Holy Spirit – an Introduction*. Mattersey: Mattersey Hall, 1998.

Piper, John. *Let the Nations Be Glad*. Leicester: IVP, 2010.

Reymond, Robert L. *Paul Missionary and Theologian*. Fearn: Mentor, 2000.

Robeck, Cecil Jr. *The Azusa Street Mission and Revival*. Nashville TN: Thomas Nelson, 2006.

Roxburgh, Alan and Fred Romanuk. *The Missional Leader*. San Francisco: Jossey-Boss, 2006.

Saunders, J. Oswald. *Spiritual Leadership*. Chicago: Moody, 1994.

Stott, John. *Basic Christian Leadership*. Downers Grove, IL.: IVP, 2002.

Stott, John. *Calling Christian Leaders*. Leicester: IVP, 2002.

Strauch, Alexander. *Leading with Love*. Colorado: Authentic, 2006.

Stronstad, Roger. *The Charismatic Theology of St. Luke*. Peabody MA: Hendrickson, 1990.

Vanhoozer, Kevin. *Hearers and Doers*. Bellingham: Lexham Press, 2019.

Vanhoozer, Kevin and Owen Strachan. *The Pastor as Public Theologian*. Grand Rapids MI: Baker, 2015.

Warrington, Keith. *Discovering the Holy Spirit in the New Testament*. Peabody, MA: Hendrickson, 2005.

Warrington, Keith. *Healing and Suffering*. Milton Keynes: Paternoster, 2005.

Warrington, Keith. *The Message of the Holy Spirit*. Leicester: IVP, 2009.

Warrington, Keith. *Pentecostal Theology*. London: T&T Clark, 2008.

J. Rodman Williams. *Renewal Theology*. Grand Rapids MI: Zondervan, 1996.

Wimber, John. *Power Evangelism*. London: Hodder and Stoughton, 1985.

Wright, Chris. *The Mission of God*. Downers Grove: IVP, 2006.

BV - #0006 - 151020 - C0 - 229/152/8 - PB - 9781913181529